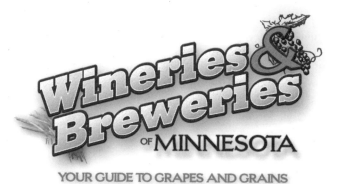

Wineries & Breweries
OF MINNESOTA

YOUR GUIDE TO GRAPES AND GRAINS

BY NORM AYEN & SHANE WEIBEL

Adventure Publications, Inc.
Cambridge, MN

Thanks to my wife Judy for the support I received on the book. I would also like to thank all the wineries for their support and enthusiasm—they made this project a very enjoyable experience. Their hospitality is truly appreciated. I wish all Minnesota's wineries much success now and for many years to come.

~*Norm Ayen*￼

Thanks to my wife Tina and son Kellen for their support. Thanks to Ben Davis for the Schell connection, thanks "Dutch." Thanks to Clifford and T. Mollert for their hospitality and stories on St. Peter's brewing past. Also to David "The Colonel" Tell for contributions to the beer tasting. Thanks to Lee Orvik for his many ideas and contributions. And lastly to the brewers, owners and employees—this book is not possible without your help.

~*Shane Weibel*

Disclaimer
If you decide to explore Minnesota's wineries and breweries, neither the authors, nor the establishments nor the publisher can be held responsible for accidents, injuries or losses resulting directly or indirectly from the content of this book. You are responsible for your safety and decisions.

Cover and Book Design by Jonathan Norberg

Copyright 2005 by Norm Ayen and Shane Weibel

Published by
Adventure Publications, Inc.
820 Cleveland Street South
Cambridge, MN 55008
1-800-678-7006

ISBN-13: 978-1-59193-114-0
ISBN-10: 1-59193-114-2

TABLE OF CONTENTS

A NOTE ABOUT THIS BOOK

The authors, Norm Ayen, wine enthusiast, and Shane Weibel, beer enthusiast, personally visited each of Minnesota's wineries and breweries. Whenever possible, they toured the facilities, interviewed the owners and sampled the wares. They were pleasantly surprised at the number, variety and quality of the establishments they visited. They wanted to share their excitement and appreciation for what they found so others would be encouraged to explore what's right here in our own backyard. In addition to the information they provide in each of the profiles, they share their own personal experiences about the atmosphere and overall impressions from their visits.

A NOTE FROM NORM

In Minnesota, winemaking has become a growing, vibrant industry. Wineries have begun to spring up throughout Minnesota bringing new business and tourism to all parts of the state.

In the southern part of the state, you will mostly find wines made from a variety of grapes. Moving farther north, more wines are made with fruits commonly found within the state such as apple, blueberry, strawberry, cranberry, plus a wealth of others. Some wines may even be a blend of fruits and honey, creating a unique tasting experience.

The one thing I found that impressed me most as I traveled around Minnesota and visited the different wineries was that everyone was so friendly. Winery owners and winemakers are anxious to share their wine experience with everyone.

I give a special thanks to all the Minnesota wineries for their help providing me with information for this book. Each winery provides a different experience and unique wines for their customers. I wish them all much success.

I highly encourage everyone to visit the Minnesota wineries. Enjoy your wine experience and remember to drink responsibly. Purchase Minnesota wines—you'll find that good, award-winning wines are being produced right here in the Upper Midwest.

A NOTE FROM SHANE

A recipe for Minnesota beer: Mix water—10,000 lakes plus rivers, streams and creeks—with thousands of square miles of fertile farmland. Add a bunch of immigrants with a history of brewing, and give the process a few years to mature.

The majority of Minnesota's population at one time engaged in agriculture. A healthy agricultural economy is conducive to a brewing economy; the evolution is natural. Farmers bring their grains to market, malting companies purchase the grain, brewers purchase the malt, then farmers buy the spent mash from the brewer to feed to their livestock. A true working relationship emerged.

The brewing tradition is Minnesota is as old as the state itself. At one time the state boasted over 167 breweries in 101 different cities. Names like Gluek, Hamm's, Schmidt, Schell's, Grain Belt, Cold Spring and Stroh's all began their brewing traditions in Minnesota. What happened to all of those breweries? Two factors contributed to their decline: Prohibition and competition. Most breweries attempted to survive Prohibition by producing candy, root beer, even furniture, but by the time that it was repealed in 1933 it was too late for most. Bigger breweries with more money pushed out or bought out the smaller ones. Today, though, there is a growing and thriving community of respected breweries in Minnesota, and interest in fresh, local beers is on the upswing.

I do not rate beer trying to find the best or worst. I simply am a fan of it. I find the variety interesting and enjoy tasting different styles and flavors. I encourage you to drink beers brewed in Minnesota by Minnesota brewers. I firmly believe the quality of beer you will find far surpasses anything brewed in St. Louis or Milwaukee. In the course of research for this book I have tried 28 different styles of beer, and within those categories have tasted 125 different beers. I have traveled over 2,000 miles on this quest and I can say it was all well worth it—the beer and the people make it so.

I thank everyone at the all the breweries and brewpubs for their help, patience and enthusiasm. Every brewery and brewpub is a unique place, but each treats their customers with zest. They are all excited to share their beer experience, and are rightly proud of their products. I have been impressed with the style and quality Minnesota brewers put forth. Seek out Minnesota beers—you won't be disappointed.

A BRIEF HISTORY OF WINE

Wine has had social, religious and commercial impact on the cultures that have utilized and refined it. At various times, it was considered a divine gift, a good alternative to unsafe drinking water, and a valuable commodity. Winemaking has been practiced for at least six thousand years, possibly as long as eight thousand. Earliest evidence traces winemaking to the area called the Fertile Crescent.

Through trade and travel, wine, grapevines and associated crafts spread from this area to other cultures, making their way along with beer and brewing into Persia and Egypt. Beer was the beverage of the workers; wine was the drink of choice among higher social circles.

Phoenician traders most likely introduced the thriving Greek civilization to wine. When the Greeks became acquainted with wine, it enjoyed a tremendous boost in popularity and status. Dionysus (called Bacchus by the Romans) was the deity associated with wine and revelry. The Greeks made great improvements in viticulture and wine storage. Different regions of the mainland and the islands each developed distinct wines.

As the neighboring Roman civilization blossomed and grew, viniculture experienced another forward bound. The Romans continued to improve grapevines and wines and introduced glass containers for wine. As the Roman Empire spread across Europe and Africa, new vineyards were planted. Those in France and certain areas of Germany gained the reputation for producing the best wines.

Winemaking did not decline when the Roman Empire did. The old vineyards in France continued to produce fine wines, and the monasteries of the Middle Ages were responsible for planting and tending even more vineyards.

With exploration, wine and vineyards came to the New World. The near-demise of the vineyards of the Old World came from this new land. The *Phylloxera vitifoliae* insect, previously unknown outside of the Mississippi River Valley, was accidentally introduced to Europe's vineyards around 1863. The native grapevines had no resistance to this insect, and over the next 20 years were devastated.

When it was discovered that native North American grapevines had a resistance due to their very thick rootskins, North American rootstock was brought to Europe, and European vines were grafted onto these rootstocks.

Unfortunately, a large number of less-popular European vines were not grafted, and so died out.

After the near extinction of Europe's vines, France's wines were in highest demand. Markets were soon flooded with lousy, overpriced wines claiming to be fine French wines. To end the string of impostors and wine of poor quality, French winemakers started a strict system of regulation to ensure wine quality and winemaker reputation. This system was adopted by other winemaking countries and is still in practice today.

In the New World, the Franciscan Father Junipero Serra planted vines at Mission San Diego in 1769. This was California's first vineyard. By 1900, America had a strong commercial wine industry.

Prohibition, officially made an amendment in 1920, came close to destroying America's wine industry. By the time Prohibition was repealed, most wineries had failed. Presently, wine is growing in popularity, and American wines are enjoying greater regard in the world of wine.

WINE AND FOOD PAIRINGS

The best advice for pairing wine and food is to drink and eat what you like. As you sample new wines, you will discover wine and food combinations that really sparkle and please your palate. For those who would appreciate more specific guidance in choosing, the wineries have offered suggestions for foods that pair well with their wines. In addition, here are some general guidelines:

Dry, crisp white wines and lighter red wines will be pleasant with a variety of foods.

Rich white wines balance well with creamy or buttery foods.

Fruity white wines are a good counterpart to foods that are delicately-flavored, such as walleye and morel mushrooms.

Sweet wines are good with spicy ethnic foods and desserts.

Bolder red wines shine best when served with red meats, charred or acidic foods.

Grapes , if left on their own, fully ripen and then ferment. On its most basic level—fermenting fruit to make an alcoholic beverage—winemaking has remained unchanged, though today's winemakers enjoy greater precision and control.

Good wine starts with quality fruit. Many wineries choose to grow their own fruit so that they have fuller control over how the fruit is grown, harvested and handled. Soil, climate and water quality all impact the flavor of the fruit and ultimately the wine.

Most winemakers use grapes, though berries, rhubarb, apples and other fruits make excellent wines. Grapes are unique in that they have the correct balance of natural sugar, acid and other nutrients to ferment on their own; other fruits need a little extra sugar, acid or yeast nutrient to cause them to ferment rather than spoil.

WINE COLOR

With a few exceptions, both white and black (also called red or blue) grapes have clear juice. It is the process used in making the wine that determines the wine's color. Fruit wines take their particular colors from the type of fruit used.

Red Wine

The color of red wine comes from fermenting the must (juice) along with the skins and seeds of the grapes. Must has to be macerated (stirred) to extract as much color and tannin from the skins and seeds as possible during fermentation.

White Wine

White wine is usually made from white grapes, but can also be made from the same types of grapes used to make red wine. The difference is that the must (juice) is separated from the skins and seeds before it is fermented, so it takes on practically no color. White wine made from white grapes is called blanc de blancs. White wine made from black grapes is called blanc de noirs.

Blush and Rosé Wine

"Pink" wines are made from the same types of grapes that are used to make red wines. The must (juice) is fermented for a short time with the skins and seeds, so takes on only a bit of the color.

Fruit Wine

Whether the must (juice) ferments with the skins and seeds or not depends on the type of fruit used. For example, must from apples is fermented without the skins.

STAGES OF WINEMAKING

Harvest and crush: The fruit is harvested at the appropriate stage of ripeness and is then crushed to release the juices. At this stage, the juice is called must.

Fermentation: Depending on the type of wine being made, the must (juice) is either fermented after it is separated from the skins and seeds, fermented for a short time with the skins and seeds, or fermented fully with the skins and seeds. The must is mixed with yeast. The yeast digests the sugars and converts them into alcohol and carbon dioxide. This process also generates a lot of heat. Different yeasts are capable of converting varying levels of sugars before the alcohol, carbon dioxide and heat become too great for the yeast to survive. Fermentation can be stopped at any point to leave the desired amount of residual sugar. Once the must is fermented, it is called wine.

Many wines undergo a secondary fermentation, called malolactic fermentation. During this stage, bacteria converts malic acid into lactic acid, giving the wine a softer, buttery texture and bouquet. For some wines, malolactic fermentation is highly undesirable.

Press: Depending on the type of wine being made, the liquid is separated from the fruit solids before, during or after fermentation. The liquid is allowed to "free run" from the skins and seeds, then the solids are pressed to remove any remaining liquid.

Clarification and Stabilization: Wine is clarified and stabilized to remove undesirable elements such as extra proteins, residual yeast and bits of fruit skin. Wine can be clarified by natural settling, filtering, racking or the addition of fining agents. Fining agents cause the sediment to settle out of the wine faster. Some winemakers leave a certain amount of sediment (called lees) in the wine, as they feel it imparts special flavor and aroma to the wine that would otherwise be stripped.

Aging: Wine is aged to allow it to reach its optimal flavor and bouquet. Wine can be aged in barrels, steel or concrete tanks or even in bottles.

Bottling: When the wine is ready, it is bottled and sold. Some wines are best when they're young and newly bottled; others reach full maturity after some time in the bottle.

GRAPE TYPES (VARIETALS)

A varietal is simply a type of grape. Within the *Vitis vinifera* (wine grape) species, there are thousands of varietals. Only a handful are used to make raisins or table grapes, but more than 200 have value in winemaking. Most people recognize a few of these varietal names.

Some of the most widely-known varietals of black grapes are Cabernet Sauvignon, Merlot, Pinot Noir, Sangiovese and Zinfandel. Popular white grape varietals include Chardonnay, Chenin Blanc, Riesling, Sauvignon Blanc and Semillon.

THE NAME GAME

After the *Phylloxera vitifoliae* insect nearly wiped out Europe's vineyards, French wines were in highest demand. Some took advantage of the popularity of French wines and passed off inferior wines at high prices. It didn't take much time for France to set up its Appellation d'Origine Controlee (AOC) to strictly regulate the naming, origin and ultimately the quality of their wines. Many other countries followed suit. As a result, most European wines are named after the region of origin, such as Burgundy, Bordeaux, Chablis, Chianti or Champagne.

America also has a system of appellations; we call our grape-growing areas American Viticultural Areas (AVA). American wines tend to place emphasis on the name of the brand or the type of grape used to make the wine. Wine names may also include the AVA or winery name.

WINE TERMS

Acidity: the acid content in a wine. Desirable acid content in dry wines are between 0.6% and 0.75% of the wine's volume. Sweet wines should not have less than 0.7% of the total volume. Wines with lower acidity feel softer in the mouth. When wine doesn't have enough acidity, it is described as flat or flabby.

American Viticultural Area (AVA): a specific location that has been designated as a grape-growing area, such as Napa Valley; also simply called a viticultural area.

Appellation: a system of naming viticultural areas (regions where grapes are grown). France was the first country to set up a strict system of appellations to regulate and authenticate their wines (Appellation d'Origine Controlee or AOC). Other countries have developed their own systems; in the U.S. we have American Viticultural Areas.

Aroma: the fragrance of the grape or other fruit that is present in the finished wine.

Balance: harmony between a wine's elements, with no single element overpowering the rest.

Body: the thickness of how a wine feels in the mouth; wine can be called full-, medium- or light-bodied.

Bouquet: a description of a wine's fragrance resulting from the winemaking process; different from aroma, which refers to the fragrance of the grapes or other fruits.

Crisp: a wine that is fresh, lively and sharp tasting.

Dry: this simply means the wine is not sweet; there is little residual sugar in the wine.

Finish: the taste that stays in your mouth after you swallow the wine. It can include very different flavors than the ones you experience before swallowing the wine. Some wines have a short finish, while others are long and complex.

Floral: wine that has the aroma or taste of flowers.

Fortified: fortified wines have higher-than-normal alcohol content because of the addition of spirits such as Brandy. Most wines have an alcohol content of 7–14%; fortified wines have up to a 21% alcohol content. Port and Sherry are fortified wines.

House style: a wine blended from different vintages that can be reproduced with consistency from year to year.

Lees: sediment that settles during and after fermentation. Some winemakers age their wines on the lees, as they believe the wine takes on favorable flavors and aromas from the lees.

Legs: when wine is swirled in a glass, the legs are the droplets that stream down the side. It gives an impression of a wine's body before actually drinking it.

Mature: a wine that is in the prime of drinkability.

Must: grape juice before it becomes wine.

Nose: the combination of aroma and bouquet; the entire fragrance of the wine.

Oaky: the taste wine acquires from being fermented or aged in oak barrels. The wine, especially red wine, can carry toasty, charred, roasted or vanilla aromas. American oak and French oak are the most widely used woods.

Oenology: the study of wines.

Punt: the indentation on the bottom of most wine bottles.

Racking: moving the wine from one container to another to separate the wine from the lees (sediment).

Residual sugar: sugar left in the wine after fermentation. Dry wines have little or no residual sugar.

Spicy: wine that has a peppery flavor.

Still wine: wine that has no carbonation; a non-sparkling wine.

Sulfites: a natural by-product of fermentation; sulfites can also be used to clean and sterilize winemaking equipment. Most wines contain very low levels of sulfites.

Sweet: if a wine is sweet (i.e. not dry) it means that there is an amount of residual sugar in the wine.

Tannin: a key acid in wine. Tannin comes from the skin, seeds and stems of the grapes. This is where the pucker in red wine comes from.

Tartrates: natural crystals of tartaric acid that sometimes form in the bottles and on the corks of wines. Some believe that the presence of tartrates is an indication that the wine has not been overprocessed.

Viniculture: the science of growing grapes and winemaking.

Vintage: the year the grapes were harvested and when the wine was made from those grapes.

A BRIEF HISTORY OF BREWING

The earliest verified records of beermaking date to about 6,000 years ago. Certain clay tablets left by the Sumerians contain a verse to Ninkasi, the goddess of brewing. Within the song is a basic recipe for beer. The Sumerians believed that beer was a divine gift. Many historians maintain that ancient peoples discovered alcohol by accident when wild yeasts settled into damp stored grain and fermented. This discovery led to the frothy, creamy suds of today.

From Sumeria, brewing spread to other cultures and was refined to meet their tastes and needs. Beer's lineage can be traced from Mesopotamia to Egypt, Greece and the Roman Empire, which stretched as far as England and Germany.

Up until the Middle Ages, brewing was the domain of women. This shifted as monasteries began to proliferate. The monasteries created nutritious and flavorful beers first for themselves, then for the public. Through this exposure, brewing gained the status of a respectable trade. Brewers began to experiment with a variety of aromatic herbs to add flavor to their beer. Some of the aromatics were poisonous; others were hallucinogens. The German Beer Purity Law of 1516 restricted the ingredients that could legally be used in brewing beer to barley, hops and water, and beer began to take on a character closer to modern-day color and taste. Fermentation was not yet understood, so lots of things could and did go wrong in the brewing process.

Developments important to brewing, dating from about 1750 on, include James Watt's steam engine, which gave breweries new power and efficiency, Carl von Linde's refrigeration, Pasteur's studies of microorganisms and fermentation and Christian Hansen's isolation of single yeast cells. Different stages of the brewing process could be more closely controlled and manipulated, yielding carefully crafted brews.

Beer has even influenced our own American history. Sailors on the Mayflower hustled the Pilgrims off the ship at Plymouth Rock because the beer supply was running low and they wanted to be sure they had enough to make it back to England. Many of our founding fathers brewed beer. George Washington had his own recipes and Thomas Jefferson and Samuel Adams were brewers. Ben Franklin liked beer so much he professed his love by saying "Beer is proof that God loves us and wants us to be happy."

THE MODERN BREWING PROCESS

Today's brewing is more complicated than the process ancient Sumerians employed, but brewing essentially hasn't changed. Basic beer starts out with four ingredients: water, hops, malt and yeast. From these four ingredients, brewers have been able to create a myriad of flavors, colors and textures. The following is very basic description of the ingredients and the modern brewing process.

Step 1: Malt. Grain is to beer what grapes are to wine. Barley, the primary grain used in malt, is steeped in hot water and is tricked into thinking, "Hey, it's springtime." Just as the grain begins to sprout, the water is drained and the barley is dried. The purpose of "malting" barley is to break down complex proteins and starches into compounds that can be digested more easily by the yeast. The barley, now called malt, can be kilned to varying degrees, which produces different colors and flavors in the finished beer. Malts also vary in flavor according to where they are from, whether it be Scotland, Ireland, England, Germany or Minnesota. The next step is for the malt to be milled (crushed or ground). Once it is milled, the malt is called grist.

Wheat, rye, oats and corn are also used in brewing, but are typically not "malted" and are called adjuncts. They add flavor or color, and can help to stabilize the finished beer.

Step 2: Mashing. The grist (milled malt) is then added to water, stirred and heated in a vessel called a mash tun. This step is called mashing, and it converts the starches in the grist into sugars. The mash mixture is then sent into a large straining or lautering tub where the husks are filtered out. What is left is a very sweet, sugary liquid called wort. Sparging takes place when fresh water is sprayed over the spent mash to extract as much of the wort as possible. The wort contains no alcohol yet. The spent mash can be sold to farmers for feed.

Step 3: Brewing and Hopping. The wort is then sent to a brew kettle, which is usually the largest contraption in the brewery. Brew kettles are generally copper or stainless steel. The wort is heated and brought to a boil. Hops are added to give beer its varying degrees of bitterness and to balance the malt flavor. Beers with heavy hops tend to have a floral citrus aroma. Hops are also a natural preservative and clarifier, help a beer to maintain a good head and help to protect the beer from infection. The flavor and aroma of hops varies, depending on where it is grown. Many American brewers use hops from the Pacific Northwest.

Step 4: Fermentation. After the wort has been boiled and hopped it is rapidly cooled and sent to the fermentation tanks. This is where yeast is added. The yeast consumes the sugar in the wort and creates alcohol and carbon dioxide. Yeast adds aroma to beer, and can impart flavors such as butterscotch, cloves or fruits. Two strains of the *Saccharomyces cerevisiae* yeast are used in brewing. "Top-fermenting" or ale yeasts require higher temperatures and a shorter time to complete their work. They form a thick head at the top of the fermentation vessel. "Bottom-fermenting" or lager yeasts require lower temperatures and more time to work than ale yeasts. They tend to settle to the bottom of the fermentation tank. Once fermentation is complete, the liquid can legitimately be called beer.

Step 5: Conditioning. After the beer's initial fermentation, it still has a ways to go before it can be served. Conditioning gives the beer time to clarify and mature. Beers are clarified by different methods, depending on the brewer's recipe and preference. Beer can be allowed to settle naturally (called lagering), or it can be centrifuged to remove suspended particles. As part of maturation , the beer undergoes a secondary fermentation. During this stage, the beer produces light carbonation, and the flavors and aromas of the beer develop fully. Beer can be conditioned at low or high temperatures, in bottles or casks.

Step 6: Filtration. The beer is filtered to remove undesirable leftover particles. Some beers do not require filtering, such as certain wheat beers. Beers that are conditioned in the bottle or cask are not filtered.

Step 7: Kegging or Bottling. By the end of the process, the beer has reached its prime and is kegged or bottled and ready to drink.

THE SPECTRUM OF BEERS:
A BEGINNER'S GUIDE TO BEER STYLES

The Beer Judges Certification Program lists some 80 different types of beers, ciders and meads. This level of detail may be necessary for beer judges but for the everyday person who enjoys a beer, it's a little much. This list is just some basics—a little hint of what you might get.

Each brewery and brewpub features its own popular recipes and showcases seasonals that fit with the time of year. Some have been different, some have been similar, and all have been good.

Beers can be classified into two basic categories: lagers or ales. From there, the variety is staggering. Flavor, aroma and color depend on the types and amount of malt and hops, and can be influenced by the addition of other ingredients. Differences in brewing time, methods and recipes also contribute to beer's incredible variety.

THE TWO BASIC GROUPS

Lagers are brewed with bottom-fermenting yeast, usually at cooler temperatures. Lagers are typically lighter in color and flavor. Lagers are also matured for a longer period of time before being served. Styles that can be found in the lager family include lagers, pilsners, bock, dunkel and Octoberfest.

Ales are brewed using top-fermenting yeast at warmer temperatures. Ales are generally darker in color and heavier or fruitier in flavor. Ales can be served much sooner than lagers, since they take less time to mature. Styles found in the ale category include ales, stouts, porters, bitters and wheat beers.

Some Members of the Lager Group

Lagers: Lagering in German means "to store." Lagers are brewed at colder temperatures and are stored longer before being served. Typically, lagers are lighter in flavor and color than other beers. They will have slight malt flavor. The presence of hops is also very light.

Pilsner: Pilsner originated in the city of Pilsen in the former country of Czechoslovakia. Pilsners are light in flavor and often a gold color. The flavor is malty and refreshing, though some can be fairly hoppy.

Bock: Bock beers are typically served in the spring. Bock is also a German word for "billy goat." (The goat features large on advertisements.) Bock beers are usually dark. High levels of malt used in bock beers give it a definite malt flavor, feel and smell. They will have a very strong malt aroma. You will notice almost no hop flavor or smell in bock beers. Doppelbock is a "double strength" bock.

Dunkel: Dunkels are typically full-bodied and complex but smooth. They have moderate bitterness and can be described as toasted and nutty.

Octoberfest: Coppery in color, Octoberfests tend to have a spicy sweetness or herbal quality. They are very fragrant and smooth. Octoberfest is a very old German-style beer.

Some Members of the Ale Group

Ales: Ales tend to be fruitier and stronger in hop flavor and less in malt. Color ranges from light to amber. Ales should be refreshing and quench your thirst. The warmer the ale, the more flavor it will have. Ales are the oldest of beers and are most popular in the British Isles.

India Pale Ale: I.P.A. was developed by English brewers during England's occupation of India. British soldiers liked their beer; unfortunately, the beer would spoil on the trip to India. Brewers discovered if they put more hops into the beer it would last longer. I.P.A.s tend to have a very strong hop flavor. You will notice a floral scent and a bit of citrus taste.

Stout: Stouts developed in the British Isles. Stout is meant to be a strong beer. Stout is dark, almost black in color, and has a thick creamy feel. Tastes can vary, with coffee, chocolate and even coconut flavors coming out. Oatmeal stout is popular in Minnesota. Roasted malts give stout distinct color and flavor.

Porter: Porters are dark in color and have a roasted aroma. They will have a somewhat chocolatey flavor. A low level of hops will finish out the taste. Workers and laborers favored these beers back in the day.

English Style Bitter: E.S.B.s are creamy and malty in flavor. Tasting may provide a slight caramel flavor in the end. E.S.B. is a great beer to begin with for those not accustomed to drinking pub brews.

Hefeweizen or wheat beer: These beers originated in the southern part of Germany. Wheat beers are often the summer seasonal for most brewers. These beers are light and cloudy in color. The use of wheat gives the beer its cloudy color when unfiltered. Hefeweizens often take on banana and clove flavors from the yeast. Though it sounds weird, throw a slice of lemon or orange into your hefeweizen; it's fantastic!

Kolsch: Kolsch beers originated in a few breweries around Cologne, Germany. Kolsch beers are light and crisp. They're not as common as other styles of ale.

BEER TERMS

Ale: beers that are brewed using top-fermenting yeast (this strain of yeast floats to the top of the container). They tend to have more range in flavor and color than lagers.

Barrel: how beer production is measured. One barrel holds 31 gallons of beer. Two kegs make one barrel.

Barley: the main grain used in brewing. After it is sprouted and dried, it is kilned to different degrees to influence the beer's flavor and color.

Beer engine: a hand pump used to draw cask conditioned beers from their casks to your glass. It relies on basic air pressure rather than pressure created by carbon dioxide or nitrogen. Also simply called a hand pump.

Body: the thickness of a beer.

Brewpub: an establishment that brews its own beer and sells at least half of it in its pub.

Carbonation: the sparkly, fizzy bubbles caused by carbon dioxide. Carbonation develops during secondary fermentation or is injected into finished beer.

Cask conditioned: beer that is kept in a cask is active until the last drop is served because secondary fermentation and maturation continue. If you have a glass of cask beer at the beginning of the week and come back for a glass later, it may taste different. Cask conditioned beers are served at a warmer temperature than most Americans are accustomed to.

Conditioning: part of the brewing process; conditioning allows the beer to clarify and mature, and in most cases involves secondary fermentation (forms more complex flavor and light carbonation).

Draft: beer dispensed from a container by use of a hand pump, air pressure or carbon dioxide injected into the container.

Fermentation: the process during which live yeast digests sugars in the wort (sugary liquid from boiled, ground grains). Fermentation produces alcohol and carbon dioxide (CO_2), as well as compounds that contribute to flavor and aroma.

Filtering: removing undesirable particles from beer. Some types of beer do not require filtering.

Grist: ground or crushed grains to be used in making beer.

Growler: a large jug used to take beer home from a brewpub.

Head: the foamy layer on top of beer; density varies by type of beer. A good head helps preserve the things in beer that contribute to its pleasant flavor and aroma. Different beers are designed to have different heads, so a range of glassware has been developed to make the most of each beer's head development and retention. These types of glassware include mugs, pilsners, pint glasses, snifters and tulips.

Hops: (primarily *Humulus lupulus* vines) the dried, ripe flowers that are used to give beer its bitterness. Hops help to balance out the malt flavor and preserve the beer.

Lager: beers that are brewed using bottom-fermenting yeast (a yeast strain that sinks to the bottom of the vessel). Lagers tend to take more time and are typically lighter in color. Most popular American beers are lagers.

Lagering: a method of conditioning beer. The beer is kept at cold temperatures and residual yeast and other particles settle out. Beer that is lagered still develops carbonation and complex flavors.

Lautering: lautering takes place at the end of the mashing stage. It simply means to separate the sugary wort from the mash solids.

Malt: barley or another grain that has been tricked into thinking it is springtime. When the barley begins to sprout it is dried, kilned and sent to the brewer.

Mash: when grist (ground grain) is stirred, heated and mixed with water the resulting stuff is called mash. Mashing releases the sugars in the malt. Spent mash (the leftover solids) is often used by farmers to feed livestock.

Microbrewery: a small brewery that produces less than 15,000 barrels annually. Most of the beer is sold somewhere other than at the brewery.

Pint: the common size of a beer when ordered, equivalent to 16 fluid ounces.

Pushed: term used to describe one method of getting beer from the cask to your glass. CO_2 or Nitrogen can be used to "push" the beer out.

Secondary fermentation: part of conditioning. Secondary fermentation allows the beer to mature and develop flavor and aroma and can take anywhere from a few weeks to several months.

Sparge: at the end of the mashing stage, the sweet wort is drained from the mash solids. The spent mash is then sprayed with water to get all the usable sugars out. Spraying the mash is called sparging.

Wort: sugary liquid that has not been fermented yet. Wort is made by soaking grist (ground grain) in a large kettle. The wort is separated from the solids and is pumped to a brewing tank and from there to a fermentation tank where yeast is added.

Yeast: a living organism that digests sugar. Also used in baking. The types of yeast used in brewing beer are two strains of *Saccharomyces cerevisiae*.

ALCOHOL AND HEALTH

Our media is awash with conflicting information about alcohol and health. One thing that seems to be constant is that if you do drink, responsible enjoyment and moderation is best. An article from Minnesota's Mayo Clinic and also the American Heart Association states that moderate drinking is two drinks a day for a man and one drink a day for a woman or persons over 65 years of age. One drink is 12 ounces of beer or 5 ounces of wine. Ultimately, it is a personal choice whether to partake in alcoholic beverages or not.

Pros of Alcohol Consumption

- alcohol exhibits some benefits for the heart; these include reduced risk of heart disease, stroke and death from heart attack

- alcohol can reduce the risk of gallstones and possibly the risk of diabetes

- enjoying a drink during a meal can encourage relaxation and aid digestion

Cons of Alcohol Consumption

- abuse of alcohol can increase the risk of cancers

- alcohol abuse can lead to high blood pressure, cirrhosis of the liver, heart failure and stroke

- alcohol can have negative interactions with some common medications and health conditions

Red Wine in Particular

Red wine has enjoyed more attention than other types of alcohol as a source of possible health benefits. The dark grapes used in making red wine contain certain beneficial plant chemicals called phytochemicals. Phytochemicals have demonstrated antioxidant properties and have shown capability in improving cholesterol levels. Many foods, including blueberries and broccoli, contain the same phytochemicals. Antioxidants are beneficial because they stabilize toxic levels of free radicals, compounds that are blamed for the cell damage that causes cancers, heart disease and age-related disorders.

If you choose to consume alcohol, enjoy it responsibly and in moderation.

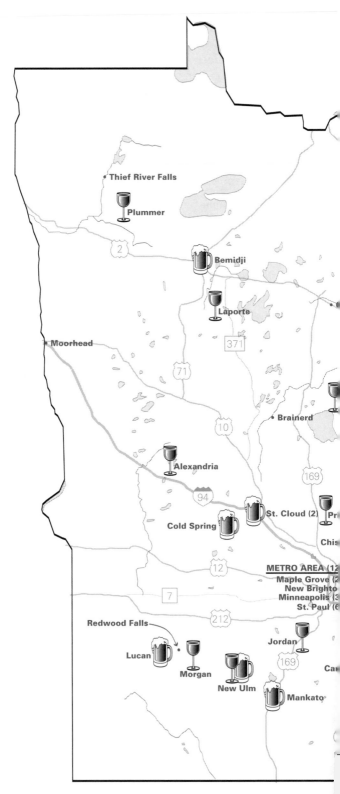

Thief River Falls

Plummer

Bemidji

Laporte

Moorhead

[71]

Brainerd

[10]

[169]

Alexandria

[94]

Cold Spring

St. Cloud (2)

Pr

Chis

[12]

<u>METRO AREA (12</u>

Maple Grove (2
New Brighto
Minneapolis (3
St. Paul (6

[7]

Redwood Falls

[212]

Jordan

Lucan

[169]

Morgan

Car

New Ulm

Mankato

22

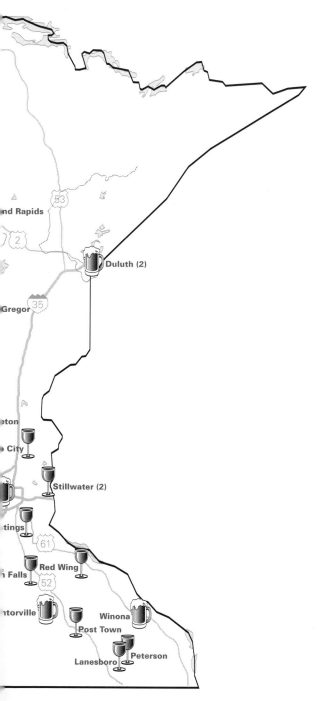

nd Rapids

Gregor

eton

City

Stillwater (2)

tings

Red Wing

n Falls

ntorville

Winona

Post Town

Lanesboro

Peterson

Duluth (2)

A L E X I S
B A I L L Y
VINEYARD

Location: Hastings (northwest of Red Wing)

Owner: Nan Bailly

Winemaker: Nan Bailly

Founded: 1973

Annual production: Alexis Bailly Vineyards chooses not to disclose this information

Price range of wines: $8.00–$25.00

Tours: group tours by appointment

Tasting: $3.00 for one sample of each of the wines made; $5.00 during special events

Unique fact: Alexis Bailly Vineyard was the first winery to be built in Minnesota.

Events: An open house is held during the first two weekends in June, celebrating the release of their new vintage of wine.

Amenities: restroom, picnic area, sculpture garden

Local attractions: historical Hastings; Cannon Valley Trail; boating; Afton State Park; golfing; Lock & Dam No. 2; Treasure Island Resort and Casino

UNCORKED...

This Hiawatha Valley vineyard near Hastings is the oldest winery in Minnesota, and it has earned national honors.

In 1973, David A. Bailly, an attorney from Minneapolis, bought 20 acres of grain fields and planted French grapes to establish a new viticultural region. Bailly chose the grapes not for their hardiness, but for their excellence and flavor in making wines.

Bailly constructed a winery made from Minnesota limestone and white pine. In 1978 the Alexis Bailly Winery opened and released its 1977 vintage wines made from 100% Minnesota-grown grapes.

As you enter the long drive to the winery you will notice fields of vines on either side of the road. Each season these vines must be buried in order to survive the harsh Minnesota winters. French winemakers have long claimed that grapevines must endure hardships in order to produce great wines. Bailly's motto for his vineyard became "Where the grapes can suffer."

When you enter the old warehouse you will see oak barrels stacked three and four high. The rows of oak barrels are like a history of Alexis Bailly's winemaking. Some bear the type of wine and vintage date. Straight ahead from the entrance you will see shelves of wines, which have received over 45 awards from numerous wine tasting venues throughout the country. You can also enjoy a glass of wine on the veranda overlooking the vineyards.

Wine lovers will not want to miss Alexis Bailly Vineyard.

WINE LIST

WHITE AND ROSÉ WINES

Seyval Blanc *(dry)* an elegant wine
Try with: fish, pesto, garlic & olive oil dishes, vegetarian dishes

Country White *(off-dry)* fruity and soft
Try with: Chinese or Indian food, salads

Seyval Ice Wine *(sweet)* "nectar of the gods"
Try with: ripe fruit tarts, dried fruits and nuts

Country Rosé *(off-dry)* serve chilled
Try with: picnics

RED WINES

Country Red *(dry)* medium-light body with a taste of cherries and a hint of spice
Try with: tomato-based meals like hearty pastas or pizza

Frontenac *(dry)* aged in Minnesota oak barrels
Try with: grilled meats and vegetables

Marechal Foch *(dry)* a medium-bodied red with lots of fruit and a soft finish
Try with: roast chicken, salmon, game meats

Hastings Reserve *(moderately sweet)* dessert wine
Try with: blue-veined cheese, nut tarts, cigars

Ratafia delightful orange-infused wine with blends of rich red grapes, tangy citrus and notes of vanilla
Try with: chocolate desserts

Miss Ratafia's Marinade

For chicken, pork tenderloin, lamb kabobs

- **1 part Ratafia**
- **1 part olive oil**
- **lots of crushed garlic**
- **a big sprig of rosemary**
- **grated lemon rind**
- **sea salt**

Combine all ingredients to make a marinade.

Address: 18200 Kirby Avenue, Hastings, MN 55033

Directions: Alexis Bailly Vineyard is located south of Hastings off Hwy 61 at Kirby Street.

Phone: (651) 437-1413

Hours: May–Thanksgiving, Friday, Saturday, Sunday 11:00 am–5:30 pm; Thanksgiving–Christmas, Saturday 11 am–4 pm; call to confirm

Website: www.abvwines.com

e-mail: info@abvwines.com

Location: Cannon Falls (southwest of Red Wing)

Owners: Maureen and John Maloney

Winemaker: Vincent Negret

Founded: 2004

Annual production: 5,000 gallons

Price range of wines: $11.00–$28.00

Tours: free winery tours; vineyard tours by appointment

Tasting: visitors may taste any number of wines for free; wines can be purchased by the glass or the bottle

Unique fact: Cannon River Winery is located in the old Lee Chevrolet Garage.

Events: Cannon River Winery hosts a variety of wine tasting and cooking classes, as well as live music and harvest and vintage release parties. The winery participates in the annual Christmas home tour in Cannon Falls. Check the website or call for dates and times for each event.

Amenities: Restrooms; the entire facility is handicapped accessible. Reserve room may be reserved for meetings (8–15 people); the winery's main room is available to rent for wedding showers, club events, etc., (50–200 people). Call for reservations and fee schedule.

Local attractions: historical downtown Cannon Falls; antique shops; art galleries; B&Bs; the Cannon Valley Trail for biking, hiking, skiing and more

UNCORKED...

Cannon River Winery is one of Minnesota's newest wineries, located in the 1920s Lee Chevrolet Garage in downtown Cannon Falls. The front of the winery still somewhat resembles the garage; once you get inside you'll see how well the building has been transformed into a modern winery.

One of the first things you'll notice is the beautiful limestone wall that dates to the 1880s. It was discovered during the remodeling phase of the winery after another wall that was used by the garage was torn down.

Another focal point is the 16-foot tasting bar, which is set apart from the main room. The bar is a nice quiet place to enjoy your wine tasting and make your purchase selections. The tasting bar reminded me of the friendly atmosphere of *Cheers*—a wonderful, comfortable bar. From the tasting bar, you can observe the whole winery, from the beautiful limestone wall to the winemaking equipment.

Also unique about the winery is the winemaking operation, which is open for public viewing. There are no dividers between the winery's main room and the winemaking equipment, so visitors can watch as the wine is being made. Next to the main room is the kitchen, which is used for demonstrations and cooking classes.

Cannon River Winery has 20 acres of vineyards in the Sogn Valley, just a couple of miles from Cannon Falls. Walking tours of the vineyards are available.

WINE LIST

WHITE AND BLUSH WINES

Sogn Blanc intense peach and pear aromas combined with a delicate sweetness
>Try with: turkey, pasta with white sauce, cheese and bread

St. Pepin *(semi-dry)* intense pineapple, apple and pear aromas, medium-bodied
>Try with: seafood, cheese

Sogn Blush *(semi-sweet)* fruity, similar to a White Zinfandel
>Try with: pasta, fish

Rosella fruity with aromas of wild raspberries
>Try with: spaghetti and meatballs

RED WINES

Mill St. Red *(semi-sweet)* light red with classic grape flavors and aromas
>Try with: burgers, venison

Nouveau powerful up-front fruit, light-bodied with a beautiful red color, hint of blackberries and cherries
>Try with: turkey, pork

Cannon River Red *(semi-dry)* American and French oak-aged, medium-bodied red
>Try with: filet mignon, prime rib

Olive Oil Cake & Frozen Edelweiss Cream

Makes 10–12 portions; recipe by Heather Grazzini

OLIVE OIL CAKE

5 eggs, separated, plus two additional egg whites
¾ c sugar
½ T orange zest, finely grated
½ T lemon zest, finely grated
⅓ c + 2 T extra virgin olive oil
½ c Sogn Blanc Wine (Edelweiss)
1 c sifted all purpose flour
¼ tsp salt
½ tsp cream of tartar

Preheat oven to 350° F. Butter and flour an 8" springform pan.

Separate 5 eggs (place the whites with the additional 2 to give you 7 whites total, set aside) and beat the yolks with half the sugar until light colored and thick. Beat in orange and lemon zest, beat in olive oil and wine.

Mix flour and salt. Beat into egg mixture just until blended.

Beat the 7 whites with the cream or tartar until they hold soft peaks. Fold into egg yolk mixture thoroughly.

Pour into prepared pan and bake, rotating position in the oven if necessary to bake evenly, for 20 minutes. Lower oven to 300° F and bake for another 20 minutes. Turn off the oven and cover the top of the cake with buttered parchment; leave the cake in the oven for 10 minutes. Remove the cake from the oven and cool in the pan on a wire rack.

FROZEN EDELWEISS CREAM

1 c whole milk, well chilled
$^3/_4$ c granulated sugar
2 c heavy cream, well chilled
2–3 tsp Sogn Blanc Wine, well chilled

Freeze bowl for ice cream maker.

In a medium bowl combine the milk and sugar, whisk until the sugar is dissolved. Stir in heavy cream. Turn machine on, pour mixture into frozen bowl and let mix until thick, about 25–30 minUtes. Add wine during last 5 minutes. Place in air-tight container in freezer for 1 hour to set, longer if hard texture is desired.

APRICOT SAUCE

1 lb. dried apricots
$^1/_2$ c sugar
1 c water

Combine water and sugar in a small saucepan over low heat and stir just until dissolved, (this is your syrup) take off heat and cool. Place apricots in a food processor and puree slowly, adding syrup until you reach medium sauce consistency. Reserve for later.

ASSEMBLY

Remove cake from springform and cut into 10–12 wedges. Serve with frozen cream and apricot sauce.

Address: 421 Mill Street W, Cannon Falls, MN 55009

Directions: From Rochester: Hwy 52 North to Cannon Falls. Exit and turn right at Main Street (Hwy 19). Proceed into downtown. Turn left on 4th Street. (Hwy 20). Turn left on Mill Street. The winery is on your left. The parking lot is next to the building.
From the Twin Cities: Hwy 52 South to Cannon Falls. Exit and turn left at Main Street (Hwy 19). Proceed into downtown. Turn left on 4th Street (Hwy 20). Turn left on Mill Street. The winery is on your left. The parking lot is next to the building.

Phone: (507) 263-7400

Hours: open year-round, Wednesday–Saturday noon–9 pm; Sunday noon–7 pm; call to confirm

Website: www.cannonriverwinery.com

e-mail: maureen@cannonriverwinery.com

CARLOS CREEK WINERY

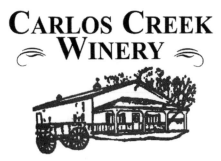

Location: Alexandria

Owners: Bob and Debbie Johnson

Winemaker: Robert G. Johnson

Founded: 1999

Annual production: 25,000 gallons

Price range of wines: $10.00–$32.00

Tours: free

Tasting: visitors can taste up to 8 wines at no charge

Unique fact: Carlos Creek Winery was selected to furnish wine with a commemorative label for the 100th Anniversary of the Minnesota State Capitol Building.

Events: The 5K Apple Blossom Run in May is becoming a large success. The Minnesota Food and Wine Festival, the largest event outside the Twin Cities for wine, is held the weekend after Labor Day. Events include the Grape Stomp. Oktoberfest at Carlos Creek Winery is held during—you guessed it—October.

Amenities: restrooms and picnic area are handicapped accessible; live music every weekend from 1–6 pm; cooking with wine classes during the winter

Local attractions: Arrowwood Resort Indoor Waterpark; Runestone Museum; central Minnesota's many lakes; boating; fishing; horseback riding

UNCORKED...

When you find yourself in the Alexandria area, make sure you include a stop at the Carlos Creek Winery.

The drive to the winery is fantastic; the lake country is such a beautiful area of Minnesota. I enjoyed my glass of wine out on the open-air patio, listening to the live music.

Carlos Creek Winery has the largest grape vineyard in Minnesota, not to mention thousands of apple trees, and is the largest producer of wine in the state. Here you will find a variety of grape, fruit and berry wines, all with their own unique tastes. They also provide personalized wines for weddings, anniversaries and other special occasions.

The large retail store offers a variety of wines for sampling, and the winery tour includes the manmade cave where the wooden wine barrels are stored. You can also taste some of the wines on the tour. Carlos Creek Winery is not just for wine tasting, though; the whole family can enjoy the visit.

Outside you will find one of Minnesota's largest purebred Arabian horse facilities. Walk through the stable and see the large indoor arena. If you are lucky you might get a chance to see some of the finest Arabian horses in Minnesota.

Carlos Creek has a paved path and two- or four-seat Italian pedal cars you can use to tour the property. Included on the grounds is the largest Siberian elm maze in the nation.

WINE LIST

WHITE WINES

Chardonnay *(dry)* refreshing fruity flavor with hints of toasty oak
Try with: chicken, fish

Pinot Grigio *(dry)* light with a mineral taste
Try with: chicken, fish, snacks

Riesling *(medium sweet)* crisp and refreshing
Try with: spicy dishes, Mexican foods

White Wine w/Peach (Peach Chardonnay) *(medium sweet)* refreshing fruity flavor with a hint of toasty oak and peach
Try with: barbecues, hot and spicy foods

BLUSH WINES

White Zinfandel *(medium sweet)* light citrus flavors
Try with: anything from fish and chicken to beef

Rosé *(sweet)*
Try with: Chinese food—it adds sweet to sweet & sour

RED WINES

Cabernet Sauvignon *(dry)* juicy berry flavors, toasty oak and medium tannins
Try with: beef

Malbec *(dry)* rustic; mild body
Try with: beef, pork, heartier foods

Merlot *(dry)* gentle, dark berry flavors with a hint of toasted oak
Try with: beef

Zinfandel *(dry)* raspberry flavors with a spicy aroma
Try with: beef

Chianti (medium dry) a fresh wine made with a combination of local-grown varieties of grapes
Try with: beef, pasta

Cuvee *(medium sweet)*
Try with: barbecued beef, lamb or pork

Port Wine *(sweet)* great dessert wine
Try with: dessert

Pinot Noir raisin-like flavors with undertones of black
cherry, spice and raspberry
   Try with: pasta, light beef dishes

FRUIT WINES

Apple Blueberry (*sweet*) sipping wine

Apple Strawberry (*sweet*) sipping wine

Tuscan Bread Soup

2 T olive oil

1 large white onion

6 green onions

2 large leeks

1 c Carlos Creek Riesling

32 oz. (4 c) chicken broth

2 12.5-oz. cans tomatoes (diced in juice)

2 T dry basil (or 1 tsp fresh finely diced basil)

1 c croutons

$^1/_2$ c Parmesan cheese

Put olive oil in stock pot on high heat. Chop white onion.
Slice green onions and leeks lengthwise then horizontally
using only white and light green parts. Saute vegetables until
soft and translucent. Add wine, chicken broth and tomatoes.
Bring to a boil. Once the soup is boiling, turn heat down and
let simmer 5–7 minutes. Turn burner off and add basil, croutons and cheese. Prep time 1 hour. Serves 12.

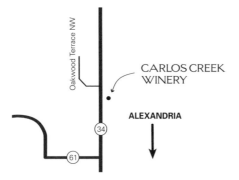

Address: 6693 County Road 34 NW, Alexandria, MN 56308

Directions: Carlos Creek Winery is located 3 miles north of Alexandria on County Road 34.

Phone: (320) 846-5443

Hours: open year-round, daily 11 am–6 pm; closed on Christmas; call to confirm

Website: www.carloscreekwinery.com

e-mail: ccwinery@carloscreekwinery.com

FALCONER VINEYARDS

Location: Red Wing

Owner: John Falconer

Winemaker: John Falconer

Founded: 2003

Annual production: 1,600 gallons

Price range of wines: $11.00–$23.00

Tours: free

Tasting: individual $4.00; group tour and taste $10.00; winery determines the number of wines that can be sampled

Unique fact: In its first year, Falconer Vineyards won two bronze medals at the Indiana International Wine Competition.

Events: During May, July and September there are music and wine tasting events. Visit Falconer Vineyards on the last weekend in September during the Studio Ramble—your chance to meet the artists and visit their studios. Make sure to check the website or call for specific dates and times.

Amenities: picnic area, restroom, flower garden (each handicapped accessible), bocce ball court

Local attractions: Treasure Island Resort and Casino; T.B. Sheldon Theater; historical downtown Red Wing; river parks and bluffs; boating; Cannon Valley Bike Trail; Red Wing pottery shops

UNCORKED...

The beautiful Mississippi River Valley of Red Wing and the scenic bluffs of the area are the setting for one of the newest vineyards and wineries in Minnesota. Falconer Vineyards is situated just out of downtown Red Wing on the hillside overlooking the valley floor and rows of grapevines.

John Falconer is no stranger to the retail business. John has been a successful artistic potter for 30 years. In 1987 he started the Red Wing Stoneware Company and built a successful business; in 1997 he sold the company to focus on his new venture of winemaking.

Falconer Vineyards crushed its first grapes in 2003, opened in 2004 and produces a variety of red and white wines including Seyval Blanc, Riesling, Gewurztraminer and Potter John's Vintage. Frontenac Rosé and Frontenac Reserve are made from the Frontenac grapes that come from Falconer's own vineyards. John adds more wines to his list each season.

Inside, the tasting room and gift area are beautifully done in wood. The antique wood stove and an old fashioned wine press add to the winery's comfortable and warm feeling. You will find an assortment of grape jellies alongside the wines.

Outside is an attractive gazebo that overlooks the serene valley of woods, the grapevines and horses grazing in the pasture. This is a great area to sit, relax and enjoy a glass of wine. The view from the winery garden is wonderful. I could imagine what the vineyards look like in the fall, with workers moving through and harvesting grapes for the crush.

John is not leaving his potter skills entirely behind. He will be creating goblets, decanters, wine coolers and more to be sold in the gift shop. As you travel through Red Wing, be sure to visit and enjoy the wine and scenery.

WINE LIST

WHITE WINES

Chardonnay *(dry)* complex and smooth; lightly oaked
Try with: pork, chicken, salmon, shellfish

Seyval Blanc *(off dry)* aromatic with a delicate fruitiness
Try with: pasta, poultry, seafood

Vignoles *(semi-sweet)* fruity aroma
Try with: crab, lobster, walleye

Gewurztraminer *(semi-sweet)* naturally fruity and spicy
Try with: spicy foods, rich desserts

Potter John's Vintage *(slightly sweet)* John's special white blend
Try with: light meals, hors d'oeuvres

RED WINES

Frontenac *(dry)* pleasant cherry aroma
Try with: red meats, beef

Frontenac Reserve *(dry)* full-bodied red; oaked in Minnesota oak barrels
Try with: red meats, beef

Marechal Foch *(dry)* fruity, lightly oaked
Try with: grilled or roasted beef, pork

Frontenac Rosé *(semi-sweet)* crisp and fruity refreshment
Try with: red meats

Chambourcin an excellent everyday table wine
Try with: light meats, pork, chicken

Caramelized Pork Loin

- 2 T brown sugar
- ½ tsp cumin
- ¾ tsp salt
- ⅛ tsp cayenne pepper
- ⅛ tsp black pepper
- 2½ lbs. pork loin
- 1 clove garlic, minced
- 1 T olive oil
- 2 medium onions, cut into wedges
- ½ c Falconer Vineyards Seyval Blanc
- 3 Granny Smith apples, cut into wedges
- 2 T butter

Preheat oven to 425°. Combine first five ingredients in a small bowl; set aside. Rub garlic over pork. Heat a large skillet and add olive oil, pork and onions; brown on all sides. Place pork and onions in a baking dish, sprinkle sugar mixture over top and drizzle with Seyval Blanc. Bake for 20 minutes. Meanwhile, saute apples in butter until golden.

Reduce oven to 350F. Add apples to pork and cook an additional 20 minutes or until pork is done. Remove pork, onions and apples to a serving tray and let rest. Pour drippings into medium saucepan and cook over high heat until reduced to ½ cup. Pour over pork, apples and onions. Enjoy with the remainder of the wine.

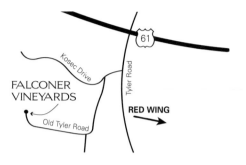

Address: 3572 Old Tyler Road, Red Wing, MN 55066

Directions: Take Hwy 61 south to Red Wing, turn right at the first stop light by Econo Foods onto Tyler Road. Turn right onto Kosec (across from Wal-Mart), go 200 feet and turn left onto Old Tyler Road. Old Tyler Road changes to a gravel road. Stay on the gravel; it dead-ends at the farm.

Phone: (651) 388-8849

Hours: Memorial Day weekend and on weekends until Thanksgiving, Saturday 10 am–6 pm, Sunday noon–5 pm; call to confirm

Website: www.falconervineyards.com

e-mail: wine@falconervineyards.com

Location: Morgan (southeast of Redwood Falls)

Owners: Charles Quast, Mark Wedge, Don Reding, Chad Reding

Winemaker: Mark Wedge

Founded: 2000

Annual production: 2,000 gallons

Price range of wines: $13.95–$18.95

Tours: free

Tasting: $3.00 for any three wines; $5.00 for full tasting experience

Unique fact: Fieldstone Vineyards is located on a Century Farm (a farm that has been lived on by the same family for more than 100 years). The dairy barn houses the winery and tasting room.

Events: Opening Weekend is the first full weekend in May; Minnesota Inventors Conference Weekend and a Classic Car Show in June; Farm Fest in August; call or check the website for dates, times and other information on their calendar of events

Amenities: restrooms and picnic areas are handicapped accessible; facilities can accommodate groups of 45 or more

Local attractions: Jackpot Junction; Rich-Ness Alpacas; Gilfillan Historical Farm; Laura Ingalls-Wilder Pageant

UNCORKED...

Fieldstone Vineyards is comfortably settled in Morgan's rural farming area of southwest Minnesota. Fieldstone was founded in 2000 on a Century Farm where once only corn and beans were grown. With the help of the Minnesota Department of Agriculture and the Energy and Sustainable Ag program, the vineyard found a way to develop an alternative crop and to diversify the farm's business.

The 1930s dairy barn has been very nicely renovated to become the winery and tasting room, which includes wine accessories and gift shop. Stanchions that once held cows in their stalls now decorate the tasting bar. Fieldstone Vineyards did an incredible job maintaining the character of the dairy barn, while redesigning the space to produce excellent wine instead of milk.

Fieldstone Vineyards has made its mark on the Minnesota wine scene. In 2003, Fieldstone won a Blue Ribbon at the Minnesota State Fair, and a bronze medal at the American Wine Society in Greenwich, Connecticut, for its Minnesota Glacial Rock Red.

In 2004, Frontenac Rosé won a blue ribbon and Frontenac Gris won a red ribbon at the Minnesota State Fair. Additionally, a gold medal was awarded to the Martell Frontenac and a bronze medal to the Frontenac Gris at the American Wine Society's annual competition in State College, Pennsylvania.

WINE LIST

WHITE WINES

LaCrosse *(off-dry)* soft nose of fruit and spice
> Try with: pork chops or panfish

Seyval Blanc *(off-dry)* a soft white; great for sipping
> Try with: scallops, pork, fish, pasta

Edelweiss *(semi-sweet)* notes of peach and clementine
> Try with: any German foods, pork, fish, fruit

Frontenac Gris *(semi-sweet)* fruity bouquet with an appealing finish
> Try with: pork, fish, fruit—a great cheese and cracker wine

New Moon *(semi-sweet)* soft fruit finish
> Try with: fruit, pork, fish—especially Minnesota walleye

Vignoles *(semi-sweet)* a lively blend of citrus and melon
> Try with: pork tenderloin or any fresh melon

RED WINES

Reding Reserve Frontenac *(dry)* soft cherry and oak notes
> Try with: red meat, game

Minnesota Glacial Rock Red *(dry)* notes of black cherry, tobacco and spice with a long finish
> Try with: beef, lamb, game

Martell Frontenac *(dry)* notes of black cherry, tobacco and spice with a long finish
> Try with: beef, lamb, game

St. Croix *(dry)* notes of black cherry and currant
> Try with: red meat, pasta

Frontenac Rosé *(semi-sweet)* bright cherry bouquet and a fruity finish
> Try with: light entrees, chicken, summer salads

Prairie Stone *(semi-sweet)* fruity with a touch of strawberry; serve chilled
> Try with: picnics

FRUIT WINES

Sunnyside Dry Apple *(dry)* crisp, youthful taste with a slightly tart finish
> Try with: 7-Up—it's a great summer mixer!

Apple *(dry)* crisp fruity flavors
    Try with: cheese, seafood, fruit

Hilltop Harvest Strawberry *(semi-sweet)* crisp tart finish, great for a hot day
    Try with: chocolate and/or ice cream; better yet with chocolate-covered strawberries

Grilled Asparagus & Mushroom Wine Sauce

asparagus spears

extra virgin olive oil

sea salt

lemon

Coat asparagus spears with extra virgin olive oil. Sprinkle with sea salt. Place on grill and remove when just starting to go limp. Squeeze lemon over top and sprinkle with salt. May also use balsamic vinegar in place of last step. Set aside.

2 T extra virgin olive oil

8 oz. mushrooms (chanterelle, morel, shiitake, wood ear)

1 shallot, minced

1 T meat glaze

1½ c Minnesota Glacial Rock Red

4 T unsalted butter, softened

salt and pepper

Heat oil until hot, add mushrooms and shallot. Cook approximately 10 minutes. Add meat glaze and wine. Boil approximately 10 minutes. Remove from heat. Skim surface. Add butter, salt and pepper. Pour over prepared asparagus.

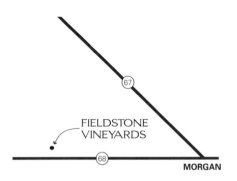

Address: 38577 State Hwy 68, Morgan, MN 56266

Directions: follow MN Hwy 68 west from Morgan for about 4.5 miles; Fieldstone Vineyards is on the right/north side of the road.

Phone: (507) 249-WINE [(507) 249-9463]

Hours: May–October, Saturday 11 am–6 pm, Sunday noon–5 pm; November–April open by appointment only; call to confirm

Website: www.fieldstonevineyards.com

e-mail: info@fieldstonevineyards.com

Location: Laporte (southeast of Bemidji)

Owners: Paul and Sharon Shuster, John Wildmo

Winemaker: Sharon Shuster

Founded: 1999

Annual production: 6,000 gallons

Price range of wines: $10.50–$12.50

Tours: free

Tasting: free; winery determines the number of samples

Unique fact: Forestedge Winery does not make any grape wine. Only fruits from northern Minnesota are used to make their wines.

Events: On the third weekend in August, Forestedge hosts the annual Art Fair at the Winery. This is a time of celebration to enjoy art, music, food and wine. Be sure to check their website or call for dates and times.

Amenities: buildings are handicapped accessible; woods walk, gardens, picnic areas

Local attractions: Leech Lake; Itasca State Park; Paul Bunyan State Park; Paul Bunyan State Forest

UNCORKED...

When you are "Up Nort'" in the Minnesota lake country be sure to check out Forestedge Winery in the woods next to Paul Bunyan State Park near Laporte. Situated on scenic highway 64, watch for the sign just 3½ miles south of Highway 200 between Leech Lake and Itasca State Park.

Paul and Sharon Shuster first moved to northern Minnesota from Iowa in the 1970s, and in 1973 began hand making cooking utensils from birch wood. In 1999, Paul, Sharon and John Wildmo established Forestedge Winery, with Sharon as the winemaker. Forestedge specializes in light and dry wines made from hardy berries and fruits.

Forestedge uses the crisp clean taste of rhubarb as the base for their unique and rich blended wines, which include strawberry-rhubarb, chokecherry-rhubarb and and blueberry-rhubarb. These fruits also make exceptional unblended wine.

Much of the fruit used at the winery is harvested on the grounds. The winery's gardens are filled with chokecherries and raspberries; even the driveway is lined with rhubarb plants. From virtually every place around the winery, I saw gardens full to bursting with Minnesota-hardy fruit.

Located beside the winery is the Gallery where you can enjoy the display of artwork by a number of Minnesota artists. In the Gallery you will find Paul and Sharon Shuster's famous Forestedge Wooden Cooking Utensils available for purchase. Paul and Sharon have been making their wooden utensils for over 25 years. Their work has been featured in *Better Homes and Gardens* and *Gourmet Magazine*, and the Shusters have won many awards for their work.

WINE LIST

Blueberry *(dry)* full-bodied red, juicy blueberry aroma
Try with: red meats, rich pastas

Chokecherry *(dry)* woodsy, after rain undertones, spicy pepper, herbs; full-bodied
Try with: grilled red meats

Cranberry *(semi-dry)* exceptional, pure cranberry flavor—wow!
Try with: poultry and pasta

Headwaters Classic Red *(semi-dry)* light-bodied balance of chokecherry and rhubarb; full of earth, spice and fruit
Try with: venison, wild rice

Plum *(semi-sweet)* fragrant plum aroma, loaded with fruit flavor
Try with: fish, fowl or red meats

Raspberry *(dry)* crisp; bursting with ripe raspberry flavor
Try with: chocolate desserts, cheeses, pastas

Rhubarb *(semi-dry)* a youthful, crisp wine, perfect balance of acidity and sweetness
Try with: fish, fowl

Rhubarb-Blueberry *(semi-dry)* extremely aromatic; mellow and full-bodied
Try with: lovely with any meal

Rhubarb-Raspberry *(semi-dry)* good body, crisp acidity, luscious layers of rhubarb and raspberry
Try with: sipping or with a meal

Strawberry *(semi-dry)* intense fresh strawberry aroma and flavor
Try with: poultry, fish, pastas, chocolate

Summer Blush *(semi-dry)* tart rhubarb start to a fresh strawberry finish
Try with: poultry, salmon, fish, pastas, conversation

Apple *(semi-dry)* light and crisp, made from a blend of Minnesota apples
Try with: cheese, fruit

Black Currant *(dry)* full-bodied red, nice alternative to Cabernet
Try with: red meat, rich, spicy foods

Walleye Cioppino on Wild Rice with Forestedge Rhubarb Wine

1²/₃–2 c uncooked wild rice (5–6 c cooked)

1½ lbs. walleye fillets (or lake trout or whitefish)

2 T olive oil

2 T butter, plus extra for garnish

1½ c onion

2 cloves garlic, minced

1 28-oz. can Italian plum tomatoes

1 c Forestedge Rhubarb Wine

1 c water

2 T chopped parsley

1–1½ tsp salt

1½ tsp dried basil

½ tsp dried oregano

1 lb. cleaned, deveined shrimp

12–16 clams or 1 8-oz. can minced clams

Cook wild rice in water with 1 teaspoon salt (3 parts water to 1 part rice) until done. Drain any remaining liquid.

Cut fish into 1" chunks; set aside. Heat oil and butter in Dutch oven; add onion and garlic and cook 2 minutes on high heat. Add tomatoes, wine, water, parsley, salt, basil and oregano; heat to boiling. Reduce heat and simmer 30 minutes. Add fish and simmer 10 minutes. Add shrimp and clams and simmer 5 minutes. Serve in individual wide, flat soup bowls. Put wild rice in the bottom and ladle the cioppino mixture over it; top with pat of butter.

Address: 35295 State 64, Laporte, MN 56461

Directions: 3½ miles south of State Hwy 200 on State Hwy 64

Phone: (218) 224-3535

Hours: Mother's Day–December 31, Tuesday–Saturday 10:00 am–5:30 pm; Sunday noon–5 pm; call to confirm

Website: www.forestedgewinery.com

e-mail: info@forestedgewinery.com

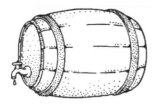

Location: Princeton (east of St. Cloud)

Owner: Myra Luedke

Winemaker: Myra Luedke

Founded: 1999

Annual production: 2,500 gallons

Price range of wines: $6.95–$8.95

Tours: none

Tasting: 2 samples for $5.00 (winery's choice), no tasting on Sunday

Unique fact: The Luedkes raise 100% of their own fruit for their winemaking.

Events: none at the winery

Amenities: restrooms; on the winery grounds are goats, chickens and ducks

Local attractions: Sherburne Wildlife Refuge is 3 miles away; one block from the winery are 12 acres of wildflowers and prairie grasslands

UNCORKED...

Established in December of 1999 the Luedke Winery is one of the newest vineyards in Minnesota. Located seven miles west of Princeton, the vineyard springs up between the corn and soybean fields of the east central part of the state.

Allow yourself time to walk around the farm and enjoy the animals and friendly rural setting. In 2003, the Luedke farm was honored by the Mille Lacs County Fair and the Minnesota State Fair as Farm Family of the Year. You'll feel welcome and right at home.

At their simple farm setting the Luedkes raise 100% their own fruit for their wine, which is unique to Minnesota vineyards. They get a variety of new cold-hardy grapes from the University of Minnesota and from Wisconsin.

The Luedkes have concentrated their winemaking efforts not only in making table wines, but also dessert wines such as strawberry, raspberry and blackberry-raspberry.

When you join Luedke's Bottle Club you buy a wine bag that holds two bottles of wine at a discounted price. Refills or the purchase of a case of wine will be discounted each time after the initial purchase.

On Sundays, there are trolley rides through the farm vineyard from 1–3 pm. Rides are free when you purchase a bottle of wine.

WINE LIST

Liberty White *(semi-sweet)*
Try with: pork, chicken; great with a meal

Evening Rosé *(semi-sweet)* lighter-bodied; black cherry flavor
Try with: beef

Morning Rosé *(semi-sweet)* lighter-bodied wine; slightly tart
Try with: beef

Red Grape *(semi-sweet)* great table wine; fruity flavor
Try with: beef

Simply Red *(semi-sweet)* dark, heavier-bodied wine
Try with: beef

Raspberry *(semi-sweet)*
Try with: dessert; serve chilled

Strawberry *(semi-sweet)*
Try with: dessert; serve chilled

Blackberry-Raspberry *(sweet)*
Try with: dessert, especially cheesecake; serve chilled

Boneless Pork Loin in White Wine

2 lb. boneless pork loin
black pepper
salt
garlic
cayenne pepper
Emeril's Original Essence spice mix
Liberty White wine

Sprinkle the loin with black pepper and salt and rub into meat. Poke about 25 holes in the loin and sprinkle with garlic, then rub garlic into the holes. Sprinkle with cayenne pepper. Coat loin with Emeril's Original Essence. Soak in Liberty White wine for 12–24 hours. After soaking, place loin and wine in a cast iron pan. Place pan on barbecue grill on low heat for 1 hour or until done. Let meat sit for 15 minutes before cutting. Enjoy the experience.

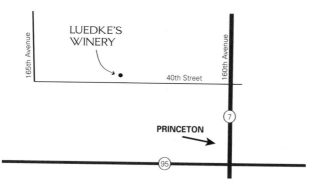

Address: 16234 40th Street, Princeton, MN 55371

Directions: from Princeton, take Hwy 95 8 miles west to County Road 7; turn right/north. Go to 40th Street; turn left/west. Luedke's is on the right/north side.

Phone: (763) 662-2389

Hours: open year-round; Monday–Saturday 1–7 pm, Sunday 1–5 pm; call to confirm

Website: www.luedkeswinery.com

e-mail: mlberry@luedkeswinery.com

MINNESTALGIA™

Location: McGregor (northeast of Brainerd)

Owner: Jay Erckenbrack

Winemaker: Jay Erckenbrack

Founded: 1995

Annual production: 5,000 gallons

Price range of wines: $8.00–$11.95

Tours: free for individuals; groups $1.00 per person

Tasting: free for individuals; group rates for ten or more people vary from $1.00 to $10.15 per person, depending on the tasting option chosen

Unique fact: Minnestalgia Winery uses 13 different fruits and honey native to Minnesota to make their wines

Events: Minnestalgia Winery hosts an open house on Memorial Day and Labor Day weekends with door prizes, tours and sampling. Check the website for specific dates and times.

Amenities: restrooms; handicapped accessible

Local attractions: Savanna Portage State Park; camping; public lake accesses; Libby Dam Park; Rice Lake Savanna Scientific and Natural Area; antique and gift shops

UNCORKED...

As you head north on State Highway 65 to McGregor, be sure to stop in at the Minnestalgia Winery, just ½ mile north of the intersection of State Highways 210 and 65.

Minnestalgia had its beginning as a shop selling wild rice, honey, syrups, jellies and jams made from fruit native to Minnesota. In 1995, owner Jay Erckenbrack began making wine. All the wines are a mix of a native fruit and honey, which gives each wine it own distinctive taste and aroma.

Wines are made from wild plum, highbush cranberry, raspberry, wild grape, elderberry, chokecherry and many other fruits and honey. These are the fruits our grandparents made their jellies and jams from, and while Minnestalgia still carries those same jellies and jams, the winery has expanded those tastes and flavors into a range of wines.

I got my first taste of this unique honey-berry wine at Minnestalgia. I was surprised and delighted by the light sweetness that honey gives: these wines are comfortable and welcoming. Tasting is the best way to decide which honey-berry wine is your favorite.

You are invited to stop by the winery and experience the flavors of the northern heritage and share in the memories of a simpler time, when all the good things you remember were at your front door.

WINE LIST

WHITE WINES

Charred Honeywine *(dry)* smooth white with a hint of classic oak tones
Try with: white meats, salad

Honeywine *(semi-dry)* white with a soft and simple flavor
Try with: light flavored foods, cheese, salad

Wild Plum Honeywine *(semi-sweet)* sweet/tart flavor
Try with: cheese, salad, light meals

RED, ROSÉ AND BLUSH WINES

Lingonberry Honeywine *(dry)* soft red; bright flavor enhanced by a dramatic fruity tartness
Try with: white meats, cheese, lighter foods

Elderberry Honeywine *(dry)* a red with bold flavor that will tantalize the taste buds
Try with: red meats, wild game, pasta

Black Currant Honeywine *(semi-dry)* robust and fruity
Try with: strong flavored foods, wild game

Blueberry Honeywine *(semi-dry)* mellow blueberry flavored red
Try with: lighter meats, salads; serve chilled

Wild Grape Honeywine *(semi-dry)* rosé with a tangy character
Try with: spicier foods, red meat

Honeywine Blush *(semi-sweet)* fresh wild fruit flavor; serve chilled
Try with: picnic type occasions

Highbush Cranberry Honeywine *(semi-sweet)* tart, woodsy blush; serve chilled
Try with: red meat, poultry

Blackberry Honeywine *(semi-sweet)* this red is the smoothest of Minnestalgia's semi-sweet wines
Try with: chilled after dinner

Raspberry Honeywine *(semi-sweet)* great for sipping
Try with: chilled on a hot day, over fresh fruit

Chokecherry Honeywine *(semi-sweet)* this red's tartness is mellowed by honeywine
Try with: sipping after dinner

Minnestalgia Chicken

olive oil

8 pieces chicken

10 cloves garlic

2 c white wine

2 sprigs fresh thyme (or dried equivalent)

2 sprigs fresh rosemary (or dried equivalent)

2 sprigs fresh sage (or dried equivalent)

2 sprigs fresh parsley (or dried equivalent)

$\frac{1}{2}$ tsp black pepper

8 slices French bread, toasted

Sauté chicken and unpeeled garlic in olive oil, turning both until chicken is well browned on both sides and garlic is toasted. Set chicken aside in ovenproof glass cake pan. Deglaze fry pan with the white wine, adding all herbs and pepper. Pour over chicken and bake in oven for 35 minutes at 325°. Place chicken on toasted French bread and pour sauce over to serve. Try with with roasted asparagus.

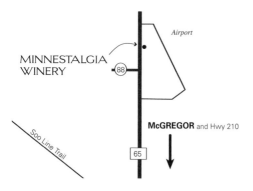

Address: 41640 State Hwy 65, PO Box 86, McGregor, MN 55760

Directions: go ½ mile north of McGregor on State Hwy 65.

Phone: (218) 768-4917 or 1-800-328-6731

Hours: April–December; Monday–Saturday 10 am–6 pm, Sunday noon–5 pm. January, February, March; Monday–Saturday 10 am–6 pm; call to confirm

Website: www.minnestalgia.com

e-mail: minnestalgiawinery@citlink.net

MORGAN CREEK VINEYARDS

Location: New Ulm

Owners: Georg and Paula Marti

Winemaker: Georg Marti

Founded: 1993

Annual production: 4,000 gallons

Price range of wines: $9.95–$17.95

Tours: Public tours are Saturday–Sunday 1–4 pm and cost $3.00 (includes tasting) ; private tours for groups of 10–25 are available May–October, call for reservations and further information.

Tasting: $1.00 for up to 12 wines

Unique fact: Morgan Creek Vineyards is the only underground winery in Minnesota. It also offers a menu of delicious gourmet breads baked in a European-style wood fired oven.

Events: Jazz night on the first Saturday of every month from May–December; Spring Bacchus Festival; Summer German Winefest; harvest Grape Stomp; Christmas Candlelight Winetasting. There is also a series of gourmet cooking classes to celebrate wine and food.

Amenities: restroom, picnic area, site is wheelchair/handicapped accessible, gift shop with wine accessories

Local attractions: August Schell Brewing Co.; Herman Monument; New Ulm; Minnesota River Valley; Vikings Camp, Mankato; Red Jacket Bike Trail, Mankato

UNCORKED...

Morgan Creek Vineyards' underground winery provides perfect conditions for the production and storage of wine as well as a unique experience for wine tasting. Entering the underground winery is like being transported to a different place. The decor is German with arched doors, wall murals and more. The winery does an excellent job of immersing visitors in New Ulm's strong German heritage.

Winemaker Georg Marti is a fifth-generation descendant of August Schell, who founded the August Schell Brewing Company in 1860. The brewery is the second-oldest family brewery in the United States.

Morgan Creek Vineyards produces German-, French- and American-style wines. They also specialize in Minnesota cold-hardy grape varietals.

In 2004, Morgan Creek Vineyards's Zeitgeist wine was chosen as the commemorative wine to be served at the 150th Anniversary of New Ulm. Zeitgeist is German for spirit of the times, symbolizing the Schell-Marti family history of 150 years and their journey from Durbach in Germany's Black Forest to New Ulm and the scenic Minnesota River Valley.

WINE LIST

WHITE WINES

Seyval *(dry)* light fruit; barrel aged in French oak
Try with: fish, poultry, pork

Gewurztraminer *(semi-dry)* exotic fruit flavors with a peppery character
Try with: barbecue, Asian cuisine; good for sipping

Riesling *(semi-sweet)* full of aromatic pine and sweet flavors
Try with: ham, pork, salads

Saint Pepin *(semi-sweet)* delicate pineapple and tropical fruit aromas
Try with: salads, fish, poultry

Black Ice *(sweet)* flavor of orange; linger on the rich body and texture
Try with: dessert, chocolate

Morgan Creek Myst *(sweet)* full of summer night floral aromas
Try with: fruit and cheese; good for sipping

Vignoles *(sweet)* rich, smooth body with a gentle pear character
Try with: lamb, pork, poultry

Zeitgeist *(semi-sweet)* luscious apricot and muscat aromas with a smooth finish
Try with: poultry, fish and pork; this is also a wonderful sipping wine

RED WINES

Saint John Reserve *(dry)* light body with a blackberry/strawberry nose
Try with: beef, pork, soups, bread, cheese

Redtail Ridge *(semi-dry)* gentle cherry flavor with medium tannins
Try with: red meats, pasta, pizza, salads, soup

Bacchanal *(semi-sweet)* delicate blackberry and earth herbal aromas intertwined with light toasted French oak
Try with: wild game, beef, pork, grilled foods

Fox Run *(sweet)* light, smooth body with fruity character
Try with: chill for sipping; fruit and cheese

Saint Wenceslaus *(sweet)* blend of cherry and Foch; oak barrel aged
Try with: great for sipping

Nova (blush) *(semi-sweet)* hardy grape has a cherry nose and a light beaujolais body
Try with: American and Italian foods

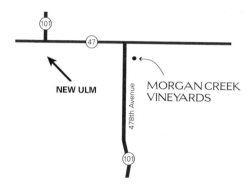

Address: 23707 478th Avenue, New Ulm, MN 56073

Directions: Located between Mankato and New Ulm. Take Scenic Hwy 68 to Blue Earth County 47. Drive 2 miles to 101 south and Morgan Creek Vineyards is the first farm on left.

Phone: (507) 947-3547

Hours: May–December; Friday and Saturday 11 am–9 pm, Sunday noon–5 pm; call to confirm

Website: www.morgancreekvineyards.com

e-mail: MartiMCV@aol.com

Location: Stillwater (east of St. Paul)

Owners: Minnesota Winegrowers Cooperative

Winemaker: Robin Partch

Founded: 1983

Annual production: 10,000–12,000 gallons

Price range of wines: $7.00–$18.00

Tours: Sunday–Friday, tours cost $2; there are free tours on Saturdays at 1 and 3 pm

Tasting: free; visitors can sample up to 20 wines

Unique fact: Northern Vineyards is part of the only true winery cooperative in the state of Minnesota. It is governed by a board of eight growers who profit-share in the business.

Amenities: viewing deck of beautiful St. Croix River; downtown Stillwater; restroom; Sunday Night music from 7–9 pm. Northern Vineyards Winery will also ship wines. Call or e-mail for information and ordering.

Local attractions: St. Croix River; parks and picnic grounds; boats; antique shops; restaurants; shopping

Events: Lumberjack Days in July; live music on the deck beginning in May; art gallery display

UNCORKED...

As you stroll down the streets of Stillwater, you'll venture past Northern Vineyards Winery on the north end of Main Street. Northern Vineyards Winery was founded in 1983 by the Minnesota Winegrowers Cooperative.

Northern Vineyards uses grapes adapted to the shorter growing season developed by Elmer Swenson, along with grapes developed by the University of Minnesota.

Most of the grapes for Northern Vineyards are grown in the southern half of Minnesota on 1- to 5-acre plots. They receive loving care and attention from their growers, which is reflected in the high quality of their wines.

In 1999 Northern Vineyards moved to its present location, which doubled the winery's size and retail area. The retail room is open year-round and features wine accessories and an art gallery for local talent.

Every 60 days the winery introduces a new artist to the public. The opening showcases the artist and the work in its unique wine tasting gallery. Displays include media such as watercolors, oil painting, photography, paper art and quilts.

Stepping into the winery from the street, you'll immediately see these displays of art. This is more than a winery; it's a place to visit for the cultural experience. On Sunday evenings, for the price of a glass of wine, you can enjoy music on the outdoor deck overlooking the peaceful St. Croix River. This is a great way to round out a completely satisfying visit. Music varies from folk and classical to blues and jazz.

WINE LIST

WHITE WINES

Chardonnay *(dry)* barrel fermented; light butter finish
Try with: chicken, pork, fish

Pinot Blanc *(dry)* hints of apple or pear; slightly floral with a long, smooth finish
Try with: chicken, pork, fish

Pinot Blanc *(dry—barrel fermented)* fermented and aged in French Oak barrels; full-bodied with hints of raisin and hazelnut
Try with: chicken, pork, fish

Prairie Smoke *(dry)* barrel fermented with hints of smoke, caramel and citrus fruit
Try with: chicken, pork, fish

Columbine *(semi-dry)* light and fruity with a hint of apricot; long, smooth finish
Try with: chicken, pork, fish

Yellow Moccasin *(semi-dry)* a tropical wine with light caramel undertones
Try with: chicken, pork, fish

Oktoberfest *(sweet)* quite sweet; exotic tropical fruit flavors
Try with: chicken, pork, fish

ROSÉ AND BLUSH WINES

Prairie Rosé *(semi-dry)* light fruit flavors
Try with: social gatherings; great for sipping

Lady Slipper *(semi-sweet)* smooth with subtle fruit flavor, good for white Zinfandel lovers
Try with: white or red meat

RED WINES

Rivertown Red *(dry)* a very soft red with deep fruit and berries on the nose and palate
Try with: barbecues, red meats

Ram's Head Red *(dry)* cedar or pine nose; deep fruit flavors
Try with: red meats

Downtown Red *(dry)* a bold wine with deep fruit and peppery raisin qualities; hint of black currant
Try with: red meats

Old Vines *(dry)* soft and sultry; slightly peppery with hints

of black cherry
Try with: red meats

St. Croix *(dry)* full-bodied with dark berry undertones
Try with: red meats

St. Croix Reserve *(dry)* oak, deep fruit and blackberry tones; superior full-bodied wine
Try with: red meats

St. Laurent *(dry)* packed with red cherry and spice
Try with: red meats

Pinot Noir *(dry)* spicy, earthy and slightly peppery with a long, smooth finish
Try with: red meats

Main Street Red *(semi-sweet)* smooth-bodied red with jam and berry undertones; great for those new to red wines
Try with: red meats

DESSERT WINES

Ruby Minnesota *(sweet)* intense flavor; some wild grapes are used
Try with: chocolate

Address: 223 N. Main Street, Stillwater, MN 55082

Directions: Northern Vineyards is easy to find; it's on the north end of Main Street in downtown Stillwater.

Phone: (651) 430-1032

Hours: Monday–Saturday 10 am–6 pm; Sunday noon–6 pm; call to confirm

Website: www.northernvineyards.com

e-mail: northernvineyards@att.net

SAINT CROIX VINEYARDS

Location: Stillwater (east of St. Paul)

Owners: Paul Quast, Peter Hemstad and Chris Aamodt

Winemakers: Peter Hemstad and Paul Quast

Founded: 1992

Annual production: 10,000 gallons

Price range of wines: $10.00–$20.00

Tours: by appointment; group tours are $15 per person with a 10-person minimum. No tours on weekends or during October.

Tasting: free, August–December 26th, 7 days a week; mid-April–July, Friday, Saturday, Sunday

Unique fact: Peter Hemstad, co-owner, is a viticulturist at the University of Minnesota. Saint Croix Vineyards makes three different wines from the Frontenac red wine grape variety developed at the U of M.

Events: Grape Stomp and jazz music on the weekend after Labor Day

Amenities: restrooms, picnic grounds

Local attractions: Aamodt's Apple Farm; Stillwater antique district; scenic St. Croix River

UNCORKED...

Just west of Stillwater you can find the Saint Croix Vineyards. Established in 1992, Saint Croix Vineyards is the third-oldest vineyard in the state and one of the most established wineries in Minnesota.

Wine tasting takes place in the 100-year-old restored dairy barn. The tasting bar and gift shop are on the upper level of the barn, where thousands of bales of hay once were stacked. The barn has been very carefully restored to keep the charm of the building and create a friendly atmosphere. Much of the original barn structure is still intact, and it is an impressive space. It might have been my imagination, but I could almost smell the hay.

Owners Peter Hemstad, a viticulturist at the University of Minnesota, and Paul Quast, an attorney, met as wine tasting judges at the Minnesota State Fair. They became friends and business partners. Combining their skills and efforts they began their own winery in the restored dairy barn at the Aamodt's Apple Farm. Paul Quast had worked at the orchard when he was a boy and suggested the old dairy barn would be a good place for a winery. In 1993 the wine was bottled and the winery continues to grow. Although located at the Aamodt's Apple Farm site, the winery is a separate business.

Peter Hemstad is largely responsible for the red wine variety Frontenac used by many growers in the state. Hemstad continues to develop new grapes for their wines. New varieties of white wine grapes introduced by the University of Minnesota include Frontenac gris and La Crescent.

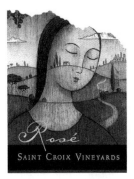

WINE LIST

WHITE AND ROSÉ WINES

Chardonnay *(dry)* delicately fruity nose, with spicy French-oak overtones
Try with: fish, chicken

Seyval *(dry)* delicate fruitiness
Try with: poultry, seafood

Frontenac Rosé *(semi-dry)* pleasant cherry and berry aroma, the right wine for a hot summer day
Try with: chicken, fish

Vignoles *(semi-sweet)* rich apricot nose
Try with: cheese and crackers, spicy food

Delaware *(sweet)* intensely fruity bouquet, a "porch wine"
Try with: fish, chicken, cheese and crackers

RED WINES

Frontenac *(dry)* robust earthy body, cherry aroma
Try with: beef, pasta

Marechal Foch *(dry)* delicate sweetness and cherry and berry aromas
Try with: beef, pasta

DESSERT WINE

Raspberry Infusion *(sweet)* an intense dessert experience; captures the rich essence of freshly picked raspberries coupled with the complexity of a red wine
Try with: chocolate, cheesecake or ice cream

Alyce's Famous Saint Croix Vineyards' Raspberry Brownies

- 2 c flour
- 2 c sugar
- 1 c butter
- 1 c Saint Croix Vineyards' Raspberry Infusion
- 1 c cocoa
- 1 tsp baking soda
- 1 c buttermilk
- 2 eggs, lightly beaten
- 1 tsp vanilla

Place flour and sugar in a mixing bowl. Mix butter, Raspberry Infusion and cocoa in a saucepan and bring to a boil, stirring constantly. Pour over flour/sugar and mix. Add baking soda to buttermilk. Add buttermilk mix, eggs and vanilla to mixture. Pour into a jelly roll pan and bake at 400° for 20 minutes.

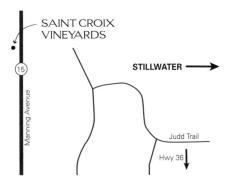

Address: 6428 Manning Avenue, Stillwater, MN 55082

Directions: From 694 E: merge onto MN 36 E (exit 52B) toward Stillwater; turn left onto Manning Avenue N/County Road 15; go ½ mile to St. Croix Vineyards

Phone: (651) 430-3310

Hours: August–December 31; Friday–Saturday 10 am–6 pm, Sunday noon–6 pm; call to confirm

Website: www.scvwines.com

e-mail: info@scvwines.com

Location: Lanesboro (southeast of Rochester)

Owner: Karrie Ristau

Winemaker: Karrie Ristau and Lucretia Brehm

Founded: 1984

Annual production: 5,000 gallons

Price range of wines: $5.75–$8.75

Tours: no

Tasting: sample three wines for free

Unique fact: Scenic Valley Winery is located in the old Lanesboro Creamery and uses only locally grown grapes, berries and vegetables for their wine.

Events: Fathers' Day in the Park; Buffalo Bill Days on the first weekend in August; Octoberfest; Holiday Open House in November

Amenities: public restrooms are available downtown; Scenic Valley Winery will ship wines upon request. Call for availability and details.

Local attractions: historical Lanesboro; Root River biking, canoeing, kayaking (rentals available); Commonweal Theatre Group; Amish tours

UNCORKED...

Lanesboro is situated on the edge of the Root River with bluffs overlooking the city: a great setting for the Scenic Valley Winery.

In 1984 the old Lanesboro Co-op Creamery was converted into a winery. Scenic Valley produces wines from locally grown fruits such as rhubarb, cranberry, raspberry, cherry and elderberry, but also included on their wine list are onion, pepper and garlic wines for cooking.

Scenic Valley Winery has an assortment of wine accessories available: everything from corkscrews to wine glasses. You will also find a very well-stocked gift shop that includes some antiques.

Be sure to add Scenic Valley Winery and Lanesboro to your itinerary the next time you travel through southern Minnesota. Enjoy the beauty of the area—and the wine!

WINE LIST

Rhubarb *(dry)* light and crisp
  Try with: cheese and crackers

Ruby Red *(dry)* full-bodied
  Try with: red meat

Harvest Blend *(semi-sweet)* blush
  Try with: cheese, ham, sausage

Cranberry *(semi-dry)* crisp
  Try with: turkey, ham

Raspberry *(sweet)* full-bodied
  Try with: chocolate, cheesecake

Purple Passion *(sweet)* great anytime; made with Concord grapes
  Try with: dessert or sipping after dinner

Cherry Chill *(sweet)* light
  Try with: after dinner

Elderberry *(sweet)* full-bodied
  Try with: pasta, beef

Plum *(sweet)* fresh fruity taste
  Try with: poultry, Chinese dishes

Scenic Valley Winery also produces cooking wines such as Onion, Green Pepper and Garlic Wine. Other wines are available on a seasonal basis.

Taco Dip

8 oz. sour cream

8 oz. cream cheese

1 pkg. Taco mix

3 T Onion, Green Pepper, or Garlic Wine

Blend all ingredients and start dipping!

Cranberry Lemonade

9 c water

9 c sugar

9 c lemon juice from concentrate

4 c Cranberry Wine

Combine water and sugar in a saucepan over medium heat. Stir until sugar is dissolved. Simmer about 10 minutes to make a syrup. Combine sugar syrup, lemon juice and Cranberry Wine. Stir well.

Address: 101 Coffee Street W, Lanesboro, MN 55949

Directions: Scenic Valley Winery is easy to find in downtown Lanesboro

Phone: (507) 467-2958 or 1-888-965-0250

Hours: April–October; Monday–Saturday 10 am–5 pm, Sunday 1–5 pm; call to confirm

Website: www.scenicvalleywinery.com

e-mail: karrie@acegroup.cc

Location: Plummer

Owners: Carol and LeRoy Stumpf

Winemaker: LeRoy Stumpf

Founded: 2004

Annual production: 1,000–1,500 gallons

Price range of wines: $8.00–$14.00

Tours: free; self-guided vineyard tours; call ahead for winery tours

Tasting: free; you can taste a number of wines determined by the winery

Unique fact: Two Fools Vineyard & Winery is the northernmost winery in Minnesota.

Events: please call, e-mail or check the website; events at the winery are still in the planning stage

Amenities: restroom; gift shop; picnic area; plans are underway for a wildlife walking area. There is also a cabin available to rent for up to seven people, which includes a hot tub. Check with owners for rental fee.

Local attractions: 7 Clans Casino; water park; restaurants; wildlife in the area includes deer, Bald Eagles, bear and geese

UNCORKED...

Several years ago, Carol and LeRoy Stumpf started their vineyard as a hobby with a love of the land and a few grape vines. That hobby has turned into a passion for growing grapes and making wine at their small farm vineyard and winery. They have put their faith in some of the best University of Minnesota wine grape varietals that were developed to survive and thrive in cold climates. They are Minnesota's northernmost vineyard, so those qualities are being tested!

LeRoy also makes wines from familiar varietals grown in some of the country's most prestigious wine grape growing regions. In addition to the grapes, the Stumpfs utilize the best of each season's harvest of fruits, berries and rhubarb to make specialty wines in the traditions of their European heritages.

WINE LIST

Chambourcin *(dry)* Chambourcin grapes are a French-American hybrid, with a flavor of red cherries, raspberries and plum
> Try with: prime rib, beef or venison roasts, stews and barbecue

Old World Red *(semi-dry)* a versatile and robust red wine with cherry and plum flavors
> Try with: pasta dishes, pizza and hard cheeses

Rosé *(semi-sweet)* a light, crisp taste of citrus and berries; serve chilled
> Try with: chicken, turkey and fish

Vidal Blanc *(semi-dry)* a floral aroma with a hint of lilac and a burst of citrus; serve slightly chilled
> Try with: salads, flavorful breads and light pasta dishes

Celebrate *(semi-sweet)* perfect for your celebrations; light flavors of pear, pineapple and grapefruit
> Try with: hors d'oeuvres, any special meal or dessert; perfect with wedding cake!

Apple Wine *(semi-sweet)* a crisp taste of apple; serve chilled
> Try with: Asian foods

Apple Honey *(semi-dry)* a delicate taste of apple and honey; serve chilled
> Try with: picnic foods, grilled burgers

Rhubarb *(semi-sweet)* a touch of sweetness is found in this Canada Red rhubarb wine; serve chilled
> Try with: fish, poultry

Gooseberry a delicate taste of springtime flowers; serve chilled
> Try with: grilled fish or pasta with white sauce

Blackberry-Grape *(semi-dry)* rich, smooth taste of ripe blackberries and red grapes
> Try with: spicy foods, flavorful cheeses

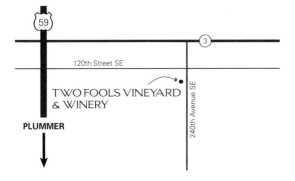

Address: 12501 240th Avenue SE, Plummer, MN 56748

Directions: From Thief River Falls: go south on U.S. Hwy 59 9 miles to Pennington County Road 3; go east 4 miles to 240th Avenue SE; then south 2½ miles.
From the south: go north on U.S. Hwy 59, 6 miles north of Plummer, MN to Pennington County 3; go east 4 miles to 240th Avenue SE and south 2½ miles.

Phone: (218) 465-4655

Hours: open weekends noon–6 pm (times subject to change, please check website or call)

Website: www.twofoolsvineyard.com

e-mail: twofoolsvineyard@hotmail.com

Location: Chisago City (north of Minneapolis/St. Paul)

Owners: Kevin and Cheri Peterson, sons Kyle and Troy

Winemaker: Kevin Peterson

Founded: 1995

Annual production: 5,000 gallons

Price range of wines: $9.00–$20.00

Tours: available during special events; private tours upon request

Tasting: WineHaven helps customers pick 8 wines to sample for free, according to the customer's preferences

Unique fact: King Carl XVI Gustaf and Queen Silvia of Sweden were presented with a bottle of Honeywine from WineHaven Vineyards in 1996.

Events: Cabin Fever Day in March is your chance to celebrate the end of winter by experiencing some of the new wines being introduced at WineHaven.
During New Vintage Days in April you can taste the new wines from new types of grapes for the coming season.
Treat yourself to raspberry desserts and award winning raspberry wine during July's Raspberries and Wine Festival.
The Annual Rhubarb Frenzy is held in August. Is it a fruit, or is it a vegetable? No matter—it tastes great as wine.
Harvest Tour & Tasting in September is your chance to tour the winemaking production followed by a sit-down wine tasting with an assortment of cheeses and fruits. (Calling

for reservations is recommend; fee charged.)
During October's Dessert Wine Experience, learn about some after-dinner wines featured with various desserts. Try the new wines and fresh mulled wine for holiday cheer during December's Holiday Festival at WineHaven. Call ahead or check the website for dates and times.

Amenities: restroom, party tent available during events

Local attractions: Interstate State Park; Taylors Falls; Wild Mountain ski and waterpark; Swedish Circle tour attractions; a garden in the Deer Garden area features two bronze sculptures of a doe and yearling created by well known artist Miles Metzger

UNCORKED...

WineHaven is a term coined by the Peterson family referring to "wine made next to our home." The manicured lawns and garden areas are very welcoming and friendly. In the winery, you can easily sense the pride the Peterson's take in their winemaking and business.

Back in the 1960s, Ellsworth Peterson and his son Kevin were commercial beekeepers. They read about European recipes for honeywine, or mead, and in the 1970s made their first batch of honeywine. The family established its commercial vineyards in 1992–1993 with Foch, St. Croix, LaCrosse and Kay Grey grapevines. In 1995, WineHaven's medium-dry Honeywine won first place at the Minnesota State Fair. A year later, WineHaven's Honeywine became the first Minnesota wine to be served to foreign dignitaries at an official government dinner. The king and queen of Sweden were served Honeywine at a reception given by Minnesota governor Arne Carlson.

As one of the top award winning wineries in the Upper Midwest, WineHaven won 21 International Medals for their wines at contests in New York and California during 2004. The Deer Garden wines, unique to the area, won seven medals. In 1999, WineHaven's Riesling and Deer Garden Blush wines received bronze medals in their respective categories. Since 1999, nearly all the WineHaven wines have received international awards.

You will receive a warm welcome at the vineyard in the beautiful lakes region near Chisago City. Be sure to take in some of their special events during the year.

WINE LIST

WHITE WINES

"Lakeside" Chardonnay *(off-dry)* bold aroma of Chardonnay fruit accompanied by hints of oak, butter and vanilla
Try with: fish, poultry

Gewurztraminer citrus & spice
Try with: spicy cuisine, seafood

Riesling *(medium-dry)* abundant peach, pear and floral notes
Try with: fish, poultry

Deer Garden Blush *(medium-dry)* extensive array of floral aromas and fruity flavors
Try with: pork, poultry

Deer Garden White *(semi-sweet)* hints of apricot and tropical fruits
Try with: desserts, rich cheeses

Ice Wine *(sweet)* exceptional balance of aromas
Try with: meats, cheeses, desserts

RED WINES

"Grapewinds" Port cherry aroma mingled with complex chocolate flavors
Try with: dessert

Syrah *(dry)* layers of complex berry flavors and toasty oak
Try with: grilled meats, chicken

Merlot *(dry)* full-bodied with nuances of black cherry and berry
Try with: beef, pasta

St. Croix *(dry)* smooth combination of berry flavors and rich oak overtones
Try with: meats, pasta

Marechal Foch *(off-dry)* berry aroma; subtle oak finish
Try with: beef, pork, pasta

Deer Garden Red *(sweet)* pleasingly sweet with intense cherry and plum

Try with: light pasta or summer salads

FRUIT WINES

Cranberry *(semi-sweet)* perfect combination of sweetness with tart cranberry flavors

Try with: a Thanksgiving meal

Raspberry *(semi-sweet)* 1½ pounds of raspberries per bottle!

Try with: cheesecake or chocolate truffles

HONEYWINES

Medium-Dry Honeywine smooth; crisp finish

Try with: fish or summer salads

Semi-Sweet Honeywine boasts a spectacular perfume of honey, which is accompanied by an array of floral scents

Try with: chocolate desserts or cheesecake

Seafood Pasta with White Wine

- 1 lb. angel hair pasta
- 1 T minced basil
- 1 T minced green onions
- 2 cloves garlic, crushed
- 1 tsp dried thyme
- 1/4 tsp crushed red pepper flakes
- 6 T good quality olive oil
- 2 T butter
- 1 8-oz. can oysters, drained with juice reserved
- 1/2 c WineHaven Riesling
- 1/2 lb. fresh shrimp
- 1/2 lb. sea scallops
- salt and pepper
- 1/4 c coarsely grated Asiago cheese, plus more for garnish

Parboil angel hair pasta for 3 minutes. Drain and set aside. In the meantime, saute basil, green onions, garlic, thyme and red pepper in 3 tablespoons of olive oil and butter. Add juice from oysters and WineHaven Riesling. Bring to a simmer. Add oysters, shrimp and scallops. Saute just until shrimp turns pale pink; do not overcook. Remove seafood from pan and set aside. Add pepper and salt to taste and finish cooking parboiled pasta in saute liquid. Add seafood back to the pan along with the Asiago cheese and the remaining 3 T olive oil. Toss well. Top with grated Asiago cheese and serve with WineHaven Riesling. Serves 4.

Merlot Sorbet

- 2 c water
- 1 c sugar
- 1 c WineHaven Merlot

Simmer sugar and water for 5 minutes. Remove from heat and stir in WineHaven Merlot. Cool to room temperature, then refrigerate until chilled, at least 2 hours. Freeze in an ice cream maker according to manufacturer's instructions. Serve for dessert or between courses to cleanse the palate!

Address: 9757 292nd Street, Chisago City, MN 55013

Directions: from the Twin Cities: go north on Interstate 35; exit on Hwy 8 (exit #132); go 8 miles east to Chisago City; turn north onto County Road 80 and take the first left onto 292nd Street; the winery is the second driveway on the left (about ¼ mile).

Phone: (651) 257-1017

Hours: April–December, Thursday–Saturday 10 am–5 pm, Sunday noon–5 pm; January–March 31, Saturday noon–4 pm; call to confirm

Website: www.winehaven.com

e-mail: info@winehaven.com

Complete information was not available for these new and/or soon-to-be-open wineries at press time. Call or visit their website to determine opening dates, hours, etc.

Crofut Family Winery and Vineyard

Location: Jordan
Owner: B. Don Crofut
Winemaker: B. Don Crofut
Unique fact: Crofut is the first winery in Scott County, Minnesota.
Events: check the Crofut website
Local attractions: Mystic Lake Casino; Valleyfair; Canterbury Park; Minnesota Renaissance Festival; apple orchards; Murphy's Landing; Minnesota Horse & Hunt Club/Bed & Breakfast; Schumacher's Hotel and Restaurant

PLANNED WINE LIST

Prairie Blanc	Private Stock Reserve Red
Eagleview White	Prairie Red
Ranko's Revenge White	Ranko's Revenge Red
Frontenac Gris Dessert	Frontenac Red

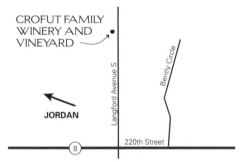

Address: 21646 Langford Avenue S (MN Hwy 13), Jordan, MN 55352
Directions: Seven miles south of Prior Lake on Hwy 13; winery is on the right side of road.
Phone: (612) 366-0551
Hours: June 1–October 1, check website for hours
Website: www.crofutwinery.com
e-mail: crofutwinery@aol.com

Diamond Ridge Winery

Location: Peterson
Owners: Kerry and Gary Lea
Winemaker: Kerry Lea
Unique fact: The blackberries used in winemaking at Diamond Ridge were planted by Gary's grandmother in the early 1920s.
Events: check the website
Local attractions: historical Lanesboro; Root River biking trails, canoeing, kayaking (rentals available); Commonweal Theatre Company; Amish tours

PLANNED WINE LIST

Blackberry	Apple
Raspberry	Raspberry-Strawberry
Strawberry	Other wines available seasonally

Address: check website
Directions: check website
Phone: check website
Hours: check website for opening date and time
Website: www.diamondridgewinery.com
e-mail: kerry@diamondridgewinery.com

Complete information was not available for these new and/or soon-to-be-open wineries at press time. Call or visit their website to determine opening dates, hours, etc.

Post Town Winery

Location: Post Town

Owners: Steve and Bonita Patton; Patton Family Vineyards, Inc.

Winemaker: Steve Patton

Unique fact: The winery is named for the small town that once stood on the site of the present vineyard. The town was destroyed by a tornado during the 1800s.

Events: check the website

Local attractions: Oxbow Park; Zollman Zoo; horse stables

PLANNED WINE LIST

Check the Post Town Winery website for wines available.

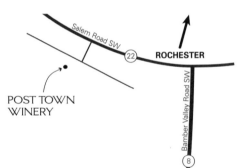

Address: intersection of County Roads 103 and 105

Directions: Go west on Hwy 14 from Rochester 5 miles, turn north on County Road 3. Proceed north 5 miles. After 2.5 miles the road will switch from blacktop to gravel and become County Road 103. The winery will be just north of the intersection of County Road 103 and County Road 105.

Phone: (507) 261-5273

Hours: check website

Website: www.posttownwinery.com

e-mail: steve@posttownwinery.com

BANDANA BREWERY

Location: Mankato

Owner: Bob Ahlstrom

Brewmaster: Dave Berg

Founded: 2003

Annual production: 555 barrels

Price range of beers: around $2.50–$3.25 depending on the size; growlers are about $7.95

Tours: given upon request and availability of brewer

Tasting: A sampler is available for close to $5.50. It includes six beers: the four everyday taps (Mankato Gold, St. Peter Red, Eagle Lake Pale Ale and Rapidan Brown) and two specials.

Unique fact: Bandana is Mankato's first brewpub and the only establishment in Mankato that makes its own beer.

Events: live entertainment Thursday through Saturday

Amenities: three bars; separate dining area; large banquet rooms for parties; pool; darts; games

Local attractions: greater Mankato area; Minnesota River Valley; Minnesota State University Mankato campus; historical downtown; Midwest Wireless Center (home to Division 1 Mankato hockey, concerts and conventions); Minnesota Vikings Training Camp; Rockin' in the Quarry in June; Ribfest in August. Check out the Greater Mankato Chamber and Convention Bureau for a cornucopia of activities.

ON TAP...

Bandana Brewery is located in the former Mankato Moose Lodge. Owner Bob Ahlstrom brought Mankato its first brew-pub and the people are happy! The brewing equipment was purchased over the internet in 2002 and the facility opened its doors in March 2003. The space went through an extensive renovation and it shows. A great atmosphere, cool lighting, hand painted murals and plenty of seating. No problem in finding a place to park. The actual bar has the different types of ingredients used in the beer set into it. Explanation of the brewing process can be found behind the bar. Large chalkboards above the main bar contain the beer menu, featured beers and specials. The staff and service are great; they are happy to answer any questions about the beer, the bar or the food. If pool or darts are your passion, plenty of both are available. Anyone would enjoy a tall one at Bandana Brewery.

BEER LIST

Bandana Brewery features four regular taps and two specialties. Specialty beers rotate as fast as people empty the serving tanks. All of their beers are brewed with Minnesota ingredients.

REGULAR TAPS

Mankato Gold

most popular, a great light beer with flavor. The beer is brewed using hops from the Pacific Northwest and barley from Minnesota.

Eagle Lake Pale Ale

excellent pale ale, one of the best this author has ever tasted. The beer has a very hoppy taste and aroma. The brewer has been working on this recipe for ten years and it shows!

Rapidan Brown

this is a traditional English brown ale. Four different malts are used to make this ale, the darkest of their taps. The beer has a sweet flavor you're sure to enjoy. If you are not a fan of dark beer, do not be afraid of this one. It is excellent.

St. Peter Red

like any red beer St. Peter Red is easy to drink. A great beer for a hot day!

SEASONALS

Waseca Honey Wheat

a honey wheat beer—you can actually taste the honey. Waseca Honey has ten times the amount of honey than other honey wheats.

Skyline Weizenbock

this bock beer is good and heavy. Weizenbock's other name is "liquid bread" because of its dark color and nourishing qualities. Who said beer isn't good for you?

BARB'S FAMOUS BEER CHEESE SOUP

- **1 lb. butter**
- **4 c flour**
- **7 c chicken broth**
- **1 pint heavy cream**
- **1½ lbs. aged cheddar cheese**
- **12 oz. Mankato Gold beer**

Combine butter and flour to create a roux. Slowly begin adding in the rest of the ingredients. Bring to a boil, and boil for 15 minutes. Makes 1 gallon of soup.

Address: 302 N. Plainview, Mankato, MN 56001

Directions: from 169: exit on to Hwy 22; head south and go 10.4 miles; turn on E. Madison Avenue and go 1.2 miles; turn on N. Victory Drive and go 0.3 mile; turn on Fair Street and go 0.1 mile; continue on N. Plainview Avenue and go 0.1 mile; brewery is on the right.

Phone: (507) 388-2288

Hours: Monday–Saturday 11 am–1 am; Sunday 11 am–midnight; call to confirm

Website: www.bandanabrewery.com

e-mail: bandanabrewery@yahoo.com

BARLEY JOHN'S BREW PUB

Location: New Brighton

Owners: John Moore and Laura Subak

Brewmaster: John Moore

Founded: 2000

Annual production: 200 barrels

Price range of beers: about $2.75–$4.25 a pint. Growlers are available for around $3.00 per bottle plus the cost of the brew you fill it with.

Tours: just ask

Tasting: A sampler is available for around $5. The four house beers are served in a rotating hopper, and each beer is clearly marked.

Unique fact: The bar was made out of a maple tree from John's grandma's yard. The stained glass in the restaurant is made by John's mom. Barley John's is the smallest decoction brewhouse in the United States. Decoction brewing is a 600-year-old German tradition using open-top fermenting before brewing.

Events: live music Tuesday, Friday and Saturday; eclectic mix of jazz, folk and Celtic

Amenities: restrooms; outdoor seating; portable fire pit— enjoy a beer outside in the dead of winter; small gardens; seating for up to 50; bar area and dining area are separate; wine and spirits and a full menu are available. Gardens provide for some of the ingredients used in both the brewing (hops and barley) and in the dishes prepared in the kitchen. Barley John's offers its customers the Barley Beer Society. Member benefits include Happy Hour prices all the time, first beer free for seasonals, Saturday Night beer special for $1.50 per pint from 10–midnight and special growler discount, which saves you $2.00 on select beers. All member benefits for $65.00 annually, ask for details.

Local attractions: Rosedale shopping mall; Bethel University Campus; Northwestern University Campus; Hamline University Campus; State Fairgrounds; St. Paul Saints Baseball; Northeast Minneapolis

ON TAP...

Barley John's Brew Pub was founded in 2000 by John Moore and wife Laura Subak. John Moore started out homebrewing, working at James Page and also the now defunct District Brewery. John also spent time at the Siebel Institute of Technology for his formal schooling. He wanted more freedom to brew the kinds of beer he thought customers would enjoy. He holds a degree in nutrition and dietetics from the University of Minnesota. Armed with a desire to offer good nutritional food and good beer, John opened Barley John's Brew Pub.

Regulars love Barley John's for the laid-back atmosphere. The pub is designed in a pre-Prohibition Art Nouveau style. Hand painted murals are featured, painted by John's cousin. Cribbage tables made from the same maple tree as the bar are available. Barley John's is conducive to a game of cribbage; have a beer and count your points. Striking up a conversation is inevitable at Barley John's. The small and cozy bar is a great place to meet new folks—what a great way to spend your evening.

The food is excellent and fresh! They feature appetizers to pizza to entrees. Barley John's won Best Appetizers in *Minnesota Monthly* magazine. Service is excellent and knowledgeable. Customers are a mix of all types brought in by good beer and food. Barley John's is also very active in the neighborhood. Their philosophy is "If you're in the neighborhood you should be part of the neighborhood." They work on different fundraisers for local schools, the city of New Brighton and the Family Tree Clinic. Barley John's is a brewpub with a conscience.

BEER LIST

Barley John's beer is excellent. John uses a German method of open-top fermenting. The beer is brewed in small batches, ensuring quality and care. Barley John's offers four regular taps. A few seasonals usually show up: Oktoberfest, Dark Night, Summer Wheat or Maibock. The seasonals change as often as possible. Beers are truly lagered, with three months of aging before serving.

REGULAR TAPS

Little Barley Bitter

English-style bitter. Definitely bitter, creamy to start, maltiness with a slight caramel flavor and a really smooth finish.

Stockyard India Pale Ale

orange color, sweet hoppy flavor, bitter finish, hops stay with you.

Wild Brunette Brown Ale

the Minnesota wild rice really adds something to this beer that makes it like no other. Hints of vanilla and almond with a high alcohol kick.

Old Eight Porter

Dark and heavy, lots of malt. Chocolate and coffee flavors linger.

PAN SEARED SCALLOPS WITH CARROT MARJORAM SAUCE ON BELL PEPPER LINGUINI

Sauce:

$\frac{1}{2}$ red onion, finely diced

1 tsp olive oil

$1\frac{1}{2}$ c dry white wine

2 c fresh carrot juice

4 T butter

2 tsp Porter beer

$\frac{1}{8}$ tsp balsamic vinegar

$\frac{1}{8}$ tsp cayenne pepper

$\frac{1}{8}$–$\frac{1}{2}$ tsp powdered marjoram, to taste

salt and pepper to taste

pinch of garlic (optional)

1 ½ tsp cornstarch and enough water to make a paste

1 lb. linguini, cooked according to directions on package

¼ c onion

¾ c diced bell peppers (yellow, red, green)

2 tsp each: fresh garlic, fresh basil and thyme

1 ½ lbs. diver sea scallops (can also use halibut, walleye or any firm white fish)

Sauce: Saute onions in olive oil until translucent. Add wine; bring to a boil and cook to reduce by about ¼ cup. Add carrot juice and butter. Add rest of sauce ingredients. Whisk together and cook until heated through. Add cornstarch mixture and bring to a boil, cooking until thickened. Add salt and pepper to taste. You may wish to add a pinch of garlic at this point. Sauce can be made 1–2 days ahead of time.

In a large saute pan, cook onions and peppers in oil. Saute until soft. Add cooked linguini. Add garlic and herbs. (You may add wine or chicken broth to moisten.)

Preheat a separate pan with just enough oil to cover the bottom. When oil just starts to smoke, put cleaned scallops in pan, flat side down. Cook until they release from pan; turn scallops and repeat. Deglaze with a little bit of wine. Cook until scallops are just tender-firm. Combine with linguini mixture and top with sauce. Serves 4.

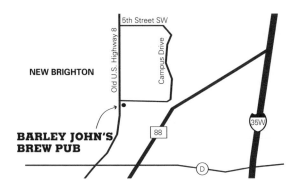

Address: 781 Old Hwy 8, New Brighton, MN 55112

Directions: From 35 W South or North: exit on County Road D; head west to Old Hwy 8; Barley John's is on the right.

Phone: (651) 636-4670

Hours: Monday–Saturday 11 am–1 am; call to confirm

Website: www.barleyjohns.com

e-mail: sorry, no e-mail available at time of printing

THE BRAUHAUS

The BrauHaus

Location: Lucan (southwest of Redwood Falls)

Owners: Dustin and Mary Brau

Brewmaster: Dustin Brau

Founded: 1998

Annual production: 150–200 barrels

Price range of beers: pints cost around $2.50–3.50; growlers are about $10.00 for the bottle plus approximately $4.50 for the beer; refills are around $4.50

Tours: just ask; it depends if Dustin is available at the time

Tasting: a sampler is available for around $5.99; included are the regular taps, plus one seasonal and their root beer

Unique fact: Southwest Minnesota's first brewpub; also Minnesota's smallest brewpub. The city of Lucan (population 220) is the smallest town in Minnesota to have a brewpub. The owner's dad makes the sampler stands as well as the tap handles.

Events: check out Lucan's St. Patrick's Day parade

Amenities: ample parking and seating; restrooms; kids' menu; great food, wine and spirits; knowledgeable staff; conference facilities and catering; TVs; gift shop with souvenirs; game room; handicapped accessible

Local attractions: Walnut Grove, birthplace of Laura Ingalls Wilder; Camden State Park; Lake Shetek State Park; Southwest Minnesota State Campus, Marshall; Jackpot Junction, Morton; Prairie's Edge Casino Resort, Granite Falls

ON TAP...

Dustin and Mary Brau started The BrauHaus in 1998. After graduating from college, the couple decided to stay close to family and bought the supper club in town. Fire took the supper club's two original buildings a short time later. The BrauHaus was rebuilt in June and re-opened in July. The brewery was opened about a year ago, an addition to the already operational supper club. Since then the brewpub has really taken off.

The BrauHaus employs a two-barrel brewing system. The two-barrel system guarantees that the beer is always fresh, but it also limits the amount of brewing that can be done. Growlers have been very popular. In fact, there is a group from Nebraska that comes to Lucan's BrauHaus annually to fill ten growlers full of their Strawberry Wheat to take home.

The restaurant features a full menu. Lunch and dinner are served. Burgers, steaks, prime rib and BBQ ribs are the favorite. Happy Hour is from 4–6 pm and includes $1.25 pints of BrauHaus brews. It is a great little bar, very unique. A super local hangout and the beer is excellent!

BEER LIST

BrauHaus uses a two-barrel system and brews constantly. They feature four regular taps. Two seasonals are offered and they change as fast as they are consumed. The brewer has total say in what the next seasonal will be, so stop in often. The Brau's beers received rave reviews at the Autumn Brew Review in Minneapolis.

REGULAR TAPS

BrauHaus Light
American light lager. Lots of flavor, nutty, excellent. About the same amount of calories as other light beers but huge on taste.

India Pale Ale
Not as hoppy as other IPAs, this one has a real balance.

Cream Stout
Oatmeal stout. Dark, with coffee and chocolate flavor, easy to drink.

Strawberry Wheat
American wheat beer made with malted barley and malted wheat. Just a hint of strawberry.

SEASONALS

English Style Bitter
Excellent, creamy and malty.

Vienna Lager
Slight malt flavor, very distinctive beer.

STRAWBERRY WHEAT BREAD

3 c BrauHaus Strawberry Wheat beer

1 c sugar

1 pkg. instant dry active yeast

9 c high-gluten flour, divided

1 T salt

2 eggs

½ c butter, softened

½ T strawberry extract

3 c wheat flour

Heat beer to 105°F. Add sugar and yeast and allow the mixture to rest for 5 minutes.

Mix 6 cups high-gluten flour with salt, eggs, butter and extract. Add beer mixture and mix for 3 minutes. Add the wheat flour and enough high-gluten flour to form a soft dough.

Knead for 5 minutes. Allow the dough to rise until doubled, then punch down and knead again. Form into 7-oz. dough balls and let them rise until doubled. Bake at 350°F for 25 minutes or until evenly browned.

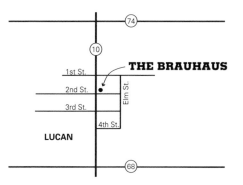

Address: 111 Main Street, Lucan, MN 56255

Directions: From Hwy 68, head north on County Road 10 into Lucan; the BrauHaus will be on your right—you can't miss it.

Phone: (507) 747-2796

Hours: Monday–Saturday 6 am–1 am; closed on Sunday; call to confirm

Website: sorry, no website available at time of printing

e-mail: dbrau@redred.com

FITGER'S BREWHOUSE
BREWERY AND GRILLE

Location: Duluth

Owners: Tim Nelson and Rod Raymond; Michael Olson, Kitchen Manager; Sheila Sutton, General Manager

Brewmaster: Dave Hoops

Founded: the brewery that was to become Fitger's was founded in 1857. The current brewery was founded in 1995.

Annual production: 1,200 barrels

Price range of beers: about $2.75–$4.75 depending on the size; pitchers cost about $13.00; growlers are around $13.00, refills are approximately $9.00

Tours: by appointment. If you can get some time with brewmaster Dave Hoops, it is well worth the wait—you will learn much!

Tasting: Fitger's sampler is a great price: seven samples (four regular taps and three seasonals) for about $5.00

Unique fact: All beers are made with Lake Superior water. Fitger's offers a full line of organic beers. All the fruits used in their fruit beers are locally grown.

Events: Fitger's hosts Beer Dinners; meal courses and beers are matched

Amenities: The Fitger's Brewhouse facility houses bars, restaurants and shops. It is cool just to walk through the building and take in the history displayed throughout. Do try and visit the Fitger's museum as well. Restrooms, elevators, access to Duluth's Lakewalk with benches. Handicapped accessible.

Local attractions: Tons! It's Duluth! Be sure to check out Canal Park, the Lift Bridge, the Lake Superior Maritime Visitor's Center, The Depot, the Great Lakes Aquarium and more. Take a boat ride and enjoy the beauty of the North Shore and Lake Superior.

ON TAP...

Voted the Best Pub in Duluth, Fitger's Brewhouse has a long history of beer making. The large brick complex on the shore of Lake Superior has a colorful history as well. Beer was first produced in Duluth in 1857 when a fellow named Sidney Luce started a small brewery close to a creek (now called Brewery Creek) near the current Fitger's site. When Michael Fink purchased the brewery from Luce, he built a larger facility on the present Fitger's site. After a few years and several owners a young German brewmaster named August Fitger purchased the operation and in 1884 Fitger's was born.

Beer flowed from the site until Prohibition. Like many breweries at the time, Fitger's was forced to produce something legal. They produced everything from pop to candy bars and made it through. The Noble Experiment failed and Fitger's was back at it, brewing the North Country's favorite bottle of suds. By 1940 Fitger's was producing 100,000 barrels a year.

The brewery closed its doors in 1972, and 115 years of brewing history was over. Enter Tim Nelson and Rod Raymond. The two owners wanted to create the feel of a Colorado brewpub in Minnesota. The new Fitger's has been in business since 1995 and is about to open its fourth expansion.

Fitger's is flat-out awesome! One would be hard pressed to find a friendlier, warmer and more welcoming atmosphere. Fitger's offers over 60 varieties of beer. They keep four taps all year: Big Boat Oatmeal Stout, Lighthouse Golden Ale, El Niño IPA and Witchtree ESB. The season dictates what the other 12 taps may feature. Fitger's has a full menu to boot! Huge portions of great food. Be sure to try the wild rice burger. The clientele is a great mix of travelers, business folks and Duluth regulars. At night a younger crowd occupies the joint looking for live music (4–5 nights per week). The pub has gone through a number of expansions and a new bar will open soon. Based on the quality of Fitger's own beers, there's no reason to order anything else. Their beers have won numerous awards. Enjoy them all.

BEER LIST

I have to say the staff knows how to pour a great beer!

REGULAR TAPS

Lighthouse Golden Ale
nutty finish, clean, a great thirst quencher

Witchtree English Style Bitter
classic bitter taste served on nitrogen—very good

El Niño India Pale Ale
really hoppy, fruity taste

Big Boat Oatmeal Stout
strong stuff, heavy, creamy and dark; excellent

SEASONALS

Red Beard Barleywine
high alcohol content, sweet and smooth, aged for a year and a little like drinking a glass of wine

Duluth Steam
bit of a peppery taste

Pumpkin Ale
fruity, thick and creamy, pumpkin and spice (pumpkin pie, anyone?), a great fall brew

Sterling Select Ale
very unique, the brewmaster's favorite. Really bitter, high alcohol content.

Hair O Monk Belgian Strong Ale
warming affect, clove and fruity taste, Belgian yeast used in the brewing

Black Paddle Porter
chocolatey tones, malty flavor, very smooth

OTHER BREWS

Root Beer
a classic root beer; great stuff

BREWHOUSE CLAM CHOWDER

$^3/_4$ c carrot, chopped

$^3/_4$ c onion, chopped

$^3/_4$ c celery, finely chopped

$^3/_8$ c green pepper, finely chopped

$1^5/_8$ T salad oil

$1^1/_4$ pints red potatoes, cut into large dice

$1^1/_4$ pints water

$^1/_4$ can chopped clams, reserve juice

$3^1/_4$ T clam base

$^1/_3$ tsp white pepper

$^1/_3$ tsp thyme

$^1/_3$ tsp black pepper

$^5/_8$ tsp seasoned salt

$^5/_8$ tsp onion powder

$^5/_8$ tsp garlic powder

$1^1/_4$ pints half & half

$3^1/_4$ oz. roux

Saute veggies with oil until semi soft. Add potatoes, water, the juice from the canned clams, the clam base and all the spices. Cook until potatoes are tender but not falling apart. Add the clams and cream and heat through. Slowly add the roux until the soup begins to thicken. Continue to cook slowly for five more minutes, being careful not to let the soup burn. Remove from heat.

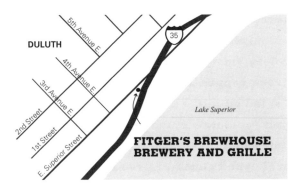

Address: 600 E. Superior Street, Duluth, MN 55802

Directions: From 35: exit to E. Superior Street; take a right; Fitger's is on your right.

Phone: (218) 279-BREW [(218) 279-2739]

Hours: Monday–Saturday 11 am–1 am; Sunday 11 am–midnight; call to confirm

Website: www.brewhouse.net

e-mail: brew@brewhouse.net

GLUEK BREWING COMPANY

Location: Cold Spring (southwest of St. Cloud)

Owner: John Lennore

Brewmaster: Mike Kneip, a medal-winning brewer of Gluek Light at the Great American Beer Festival in Denver, Colorado

Founded: 1857

Annual production: 59,000 barrels

Price range of beers: a case of 24 cans costs about $7.99 and up

Tours: full tour of the brewery, brew process and bottling/packaging facilities offered 9 am–4 pm Monday–Friday; for parties of five or more please call ahead

Tasting: four taps in the hospitality room; you can sample Stite, Stite Light, Marzen and Honey Bock for no cost

Unique fact: Gluek is the only brewery in the U.S. that does not have to treat its water prior to the brewing process. The water source is deep in the ground, percolated through the perfect granite of Stearns County. Gluek was a beer before Minnesota reached statehood. Gluek is best known for Gluek Stite, the little eight-ounce can.

Events: Gluek has local events monthly. Your best bet is to call or check the website to see what's going on. Annual events in the community are Hometown Pride Days, held the third weekend in July, and Parish Festival held in August. At both events Gluek provides beverages.

Amenities: hospitality room; restrooms; small picnic area outside of the main office; souvenirs include hats, beer coolers, shirts and glasses

Local attractions: Cold Spring Granite Company; Cold Spring Bakery; Blue Heron Rookery, home of one of the largest Blue Heron nesting spots in the U.S.; plenty of lakes for fishing, swimming and boating; great golf courses

ON TAP...

The Gluek Brewing Company is one of the oldest breweries in the state; its history is a Minnesota original. It started when a 29-year-old German immigrant named Gottlieb Gluek opened the Mississippi Brewing Company on the corner of 20th and Marshall in northeast Minneapolis in 1857. He soon changed the name to Gluek Brewing. His highly successful brewery was in continuous operation until 1964; by that time, it had become the longest-operating business in the Minneapolis area. Gluek Brewing produced beer for over 100 years and survived the Depression and a fire that gutted the brewery in 1880. During their time in Minneapolis, the Gluek family witnessed their brewery's growth from 3,996 barrels in 1858 to 150,000 barrels by 1901. Production in Gottlieb's little brewery was second only to the Hamm's Brewery of St. Paul and the Minneapolis Brewing Company, which later became Grain Belt Brewing.

The Gluek Brewing Company was a leader in beer development. They were one of the first breweries to use cans to package beer—the Gluek cone-top can is a sought-after collectible. Gluek Brewing also developed one of the first light beers with the introduction of Gluek Stite.

In 1964 the Gluek family was bought out by the G. Heileman Brewing Company. In 1966, the old brewery was torn down. For many years the Gluek brand name jumped around, was put to rest, reintroduced, then in 1997 found a home in Cold Spring, Minnesota, at the Cold Spring Brewery.

The Cold Spring Brewery also has a rich brewing history. It was founded in 1874 and was in operation until Prohibition. It restarted its production in 1933, much to everyone's enjoyment. The brewery closed in the 1990s only to be bought and reopened by the Gluek Brewing Company.

Today the Gluek Brewery is the busiest brewer in Minnesota, although most of its production is given to contract brewing of beer and a large selection of energy drinks. Their beers have won several competitions around the country. Recently Gluek Brewing has signed a deal with WCCO radio and the Minnesota Twins as their official beer.

BEER LIST

Gluek Golden Pilsner
a basic pilsner style beer—the dominant American beer; clean finish for the everyday beer drinker

Gluek Golden Pilsner Light
a lower-calorie version of the original Golden

Gluek Honey Bock
not your traditional bock beer, it has a hint of roasted malt to give a dark color; the honey adds a nice sweetness to smooth things out

Gluek Stite and Stite Light
the little beer with a punch; The beer was invented by Alvin Gluek in the 1940s and has its own patent (no. 2,442,806). A very refreshing beer. Medal winner in 1951 as America's finest malt beverage.

GLUEK HONEY BOCK BRATS

3 bottles Gluek Honey Bock

1 white onion

2 tsp butter

brats

Mix the Gluek Honey Bock, onion and butter in a pot and warm over medium heat. Reduce heat to low. Add brats and cook for 20 minutes. Grill brats until brown and serve with cooked onion slices from the mixture.

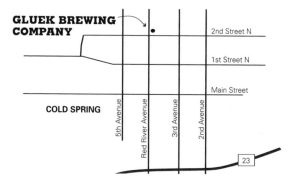

Address: 219 Red River Avenue N, Cold Spring, MN 56320

Directions: Off of Hwy 23 (about 10 minutes south-southwest of St. Cloud). Head north on County Road 2 (Red River Avenue) for about 3 blocks; you will see the Gluek Beer sign on the west side of the road. Go into the office for tours.

Phone: (320) 685-8686

Hours: Monday–Friday 9 am–4 pm; call to confirm

Website: www.gluek.com

e-mail: info@gluek.com

GRANITE CITY FOOD AND BREWERY

Location: St. Cloud and Maple Grove

Owners: Steve Wagenheim and William Burdick

Brewmaster: Bob McKenzie

Founded: 1999

Annual production: 850 barrels at Granite City's St. Cloud location

Price range of beers: 20-oz. taps are around $3.50. Growlers are approximately $25.00 and about $8.00 per refill

Tours: just ask; if the brewmaster is not there, the managers are very knowledgeable about the brewing process

Tasting: a sampler is available for $3.25. Included are the four regular taps: Northern Lights Lager, Brother Benedicts Mai Bock, Duke of Wellington I.P.A. and Broadaxe Stout. Seasonals may also be included. Samples of cask drawn beers are only available at the St. Cloud location.

Unique fact: Although the company has branches in several states it draws its name (Granite City) from the city of St. Cloud, Minnesota, which is famous for its quarries.

Events: Granite City offers its customers a mug club. For a $10.00 annual fee members get a discounts on food and drinks. Plus a few times a year a Mug Club party is held at the restaurant in their honor. On Wednesday nights, live music is featured at the brewery.

Amenities: plenty of seating and parking; large round full service bar in the middle of the building; a full service menu and wide range of wines and spirits. Customers are always within sight of a bank of four big screen TVs. Dining area is separate from the bar area. Family friendly to boot, Granite City has a full kids' menu. Outdoor seating also available. Everything is handicapped friendly.

Local attractions: located right next to St. Cloud's shopping district and the Crossroads Mall

ON TAP...

Granite City Food and Brewery opened its first site in St. Cloud, Minnesota, in 1999. The establishment featured great food at great prices, hand-crafted beers and a commitment to service. Simply put, it is a great place. The idea has caught on; since then, Granite City has opened eight more stores in five different states and three more are on the way. The atmosphere is big. Tall ceilings, tile floors, big seats and chairs, dark colors and great lighting all lend to the welcoming atmosphere. The food is truly midwestern: plenty of it at a reasonable price. The menu features everything from appetizers to entrees. Look for the beer guide to match the food with the beer. The service is excellent, and the attentive employees will be right there with questions and suggestions the minute you're seated. Owners Steve Wagenheim and William Burdick really have a winning concept and it shows.

Granite City's beers can be found at many beer festivals. They have won numerous awards and a gold medal for their Pilsen at the Madison, Wisconsin, beer festival.

BEER LIST

other offerings you may find: Oktoberfest, Honey Wheat, Yellow Fever Lemonade, Apricot Ale, Raspberry Wheat, Applecot

REGULAR TAPS

Northern Lights Lager
lightest beer and their best seller. Creamy and smooth, a great everyday beer.

Brother Benedicts Mai Bock
German-style lager. A little darker than the Northern Lights. Roasted malt gives a red color, very refreshing.

Duke of Wellington India Pale Ale
hoppy flavor, very good IPA really grows on you

Broadaxe Stout
clean and bitter, not as heavy as a traditional stout

SEASONALS

Pride of Pilsen
Czech-style pilsner. Very hoppy, 6% alcohol. Sweet and excellent, very interesting flavor, order if it's offered.

Piper Doon Scotch Ale
excellent, fabulous, stupendous, roasty, malty, smooth and bitter

CASK POURED

Duke of Wellington
cask poured, definitely a different flavor given the temperature

Piper Doon Scotch Ale
ale flavor accentuated because of the warmer temp

GRANITE CITY ALE AND CHEDDAR

2 gallons water

½ lb. chicken base

2½ bay leaves

1½ T granulated garlic

1½ T onion powder

1½ tsp white pepper

½ c Worcestershire sauce

1 oz. tabasco

2½ lbs. roux

5 lbs. shredded cheddar

2 qts. Northern Lights Beer

1 gallon whipping cream

½ c parsley flakes

Combine water, chicken base, bay leaves, garlic, onion powder, white pepper, Worcestershire sauce and tabasco and bring to boil. Thicken soup with roux. Add cheese and stir until melted, then add beer and finally cream. After the soup has been finished and before adding parsley, strain the soup through a china cap and into a second pot. After straining, add parsley and stir into soup for color. Makes about 5 gallons.

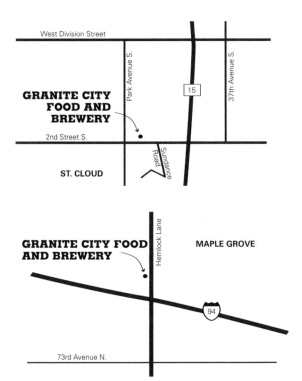

Address: St. Cloud location; 3945 2nd Street S, St. Cloud, MN 56301

Maple Grove location; 11909 Main Street N, Maple Grove, MN 55369

Directions: St. Cloud location; From 94: exit on Hwy 15; head north into St. Cloud. Turn left at the first stop light (2nd Street); Granite City is on the right. From Division: exit on Hwy 15; head south. Turn right at the first stop light (2nd Street); Granite City is on the right.

Maple Grove location; From 94: exit on Hemlock Lane (you should be able to see Granite City from here); go north at the stop light; get in the far left lane; take a left at the next stop light.

Phone: St. Cloud location; (320) 203-9000

Maple Grove location; (763) 416-0010

Hours: Monday–Saturday 11 am–1 am, Sunday 10 am–midnight; Happy Hour is Monday–Friday 4–6 pm, and all week from 9 pm–close; call to confirm

Website: www.gcfb.net

e-mail: stcloud@gcfb.net; maplegrove@gcfb.net

GREAT WATERS BREWING COMPANY

Location: St. Paul

Owner: Sean O'Byrne

Brewmaster: Bob DuVernois

Founded: 1997

Annual production: 325 barrels

Price range of beers: about $3.75 per pint. Growlers are available for around $13, refills are approximately $8

Tours: just ask, though making an appointment is best

Tasting: samples of all nine of Great Waters' beers are available for around $8; this is a great introduction to different beers

Unique fact: Great Waters is the only brewery in Minnesota to focus on cask conditioned beer. It is ranked as the 42nd best brewpub in the U.S. by beeradvocate.com, a prestigious beer information site.

Events: Happy Hour Monday–Friday 3:30–6:30 pm and 10 pm–close; daily specials Sunday–Thursday

Amenities: outdoor seating; separate bar; dining area; full menu plus wine and spirits. Great Waters Banquet Room available for groups up to 300. Restrooms are located in the Hamm Building; get a key from the bar.

Local attractions: downtown St. Paul theaters; Xcel Energy Center; museums, etc.

ON TAP...

The pub has a great vibe. It is very open with huge windows to watch the downtown pedestrian traffic. Very laid-back atmosphere; a great place to kick back with a glass a suds. The brewery is in full view behind the bar, so you can see the big, beautiful copper kettles. The brew pub required major renovations to the space, but the renovations uncovered original terrazzo floors. The beer is made using the original well of pure mineral water, which needs no treatment, under the Hamm Building.

Great Waters Brewing Company opened in 1997. By good fortune the brewery was opened in the historic Hamm Building. The Hamm family still owns the building, even though they no longer brew beer. Those who remember the "Land of Sky Blue Waters" jingle will recognize the name.

Great Waters offers two different styles of beers. The first is pushed beer. Pushed beers are beers that have carbon dioxide pushed into them as they're drawn through the lines; these beers are served cold at 38° Fahrenheit. Most American beers are the pushed type. The second type is cask conditioned beer. Cask conditioned are quite common in England and Europe. The beer is pulled from the barrels using a beer engine. A very simple machine, the beer engine forces air into the barrel, which pushes the beer out; no carbonation is added. The interesting characteristic of cask conditioned beers is that the beer continues to ferment in the barrel. The result is that if you have a glass on Monday and then return for another one on Friday, the beer will have a slightly different taste. What you will also notice is that cask conditioned beers, which are served at a warmer temperature, have a wider variety of flavors in a sip than do the pushed beers.

The Great Waters beer menu offers a wide variety of delicious beers. One of those beers—Old Bastard English Ale—was honored with a gold medal at the Real Ale Festival in Chicago. According to the owner, the brewpub has become a haunt for English travelers looking for a beer that is close to home. English or not, you will love the beer at Great Waters.

BEER LIST

Some of the beers offered are available seasonally; barrels of cask conditioned beer are changed frequently. Stop in or check the website to see what's available now.

Hefeweizen
pushed wheat beer; a true wheat beer. Cloudy golden orange color. Begins with a nutty banana flavor and has a smooth finish. Perfect summertime beer.

Brown Trout Brown Ale
pushed English ale. Malty, light hop flavor; finishes smooth. Slight nutty finish. Great anytime day or night.

Minnesota Mild
seasonal; pushed English dark. Mild, very creamy, unlike anything I have ever had. Incredible.

Golden Prairie Blond Ale
pushed ale. Very light, thirst quenching, very smooth. We tried it in July and it was perfect for the season. Good stuff!

Saint Peter Pale Ale
pushed pale ale. Sweet and hoppy, like a pale should taste. Smooth finish.

Scotch Ale
not for the faint of heart! Alcohol content is high—definitely a beer with a kick. Flavor has a hint of smokiness.

Martins Bitter
Yorkshire-style bitter. Very floral and fruity flavor, reminded me of orange soda pop for some reason.

Pot Hole Porter
very malty. Can taste the alcohol, but not as powerful as the Scotch Ale.

Anchorhead India Pale Ale
this is an IPA for the masses; absolutely delicious. More flavor than any other IPA I have ever tasted, great smooth finish.

GREAT WATERS BREWING COMPANY BEER MUSTARD

2³⁄₄ c whole grain mustard

1 c Great Waters pale ale

¹⁄₂ c honey

¹⁄₃ c molasses

1 c yellow mustard

Combine all ingredients into a mixing bowl with a whisk. Chill 6 hours before serving. Great with chicken wings or brushed on grilled chicken or pork tenderloin. Makes 5 cups.

Address: 426 Saint Peter Street, St. Paul, MN 55102-1105

Directions: From 94 W: Take the 6th Street exit; go straight for 8 blocks; turn right onto Wabasha Street; turn left onto 7th Street; turn left onto St. Peter Street; Brew Pub ¹⁄₂ block on your left

From 94 E: Take the 10th Street exit; follow straight; turn right onto St. Peter Street; Brew Pub will be 4¹⁄₂ blocks on your left

From 35E N: Take the 11th Street exit; turn right onto St. Peter Street; go straight 3¹⁄₂ blocks; Brew Pub on your left

From 35E S: Take the Wacouta Street exit; turn right onto 7th Street; follow straight for 7 blocks; turn left onto St. Peter Street; Brew Pub ¹⁄₂ block on your left

Phone: (651) 224-BREW [(651) 224-2739]

Hours: Monday–Saturday 11 am–1 am; Sundays noon–midnight; Happy Hour is from 3:30–6:30 pm; call to confirm

Website: www.greatwatersbc.com

e-mail: sean@greatwatersbc.com

GREEN MILL
BREWING COMPANY

Location: St. Paul

Owners: Green Mill, Inc.

Brewmaster: Ron Flett, who has been brewing for nine years and started at James Page

Founded: 1930s

Annual production: 400 barrels

Price range of beers: close to $3.95 per pint

Tours: you bet, just ask

Tasting: a sampler of six beers is available for about $5.95

Unique fact: Green Mill has won more than 30 awards in the past 30 years for their line of pizzas—a great accompaniment to their beers.

Events: "Roll Out the Barrel Night" Green Mill introduces a different beer every six weeks. A pizza and wing buffet is offered, along with drawings and specials on beer. Call ahead if you're interested.

Amenities: separate bar; dining area; restrooms; handicapped accessible

Local attractions: Grand Avenue, a really cool neighborhood of unique shops

ON TAP...

The Twin Cities' favorite pizza joint started in St. Paul as a soda fountain during the 30s. According to the Green Mill website the original restaurant featured "chow mein for 40 cents and lobster for 65." In 1975 the current owners (Chris Bangs, Larry Cardoni and David Bicanich) purchased the restaurant. The following years saw the introduction of their famous pizza and new franchises. Green Mill, Inc. has expanded to over 35 restaurants in five states and has gathered an impressive amount of awards for its pizza over the past 30 years; awards for their beer to follow!

Like any Green Mill restaurant it smells awesome when you walk through the doors. The pub is finished in dark wood accentuated by large windows and a skylight in the bar area. A very relaxing atmosphere. The brewery is located directly behind the bar. A small window allows you to see the brewmaster at work. Green Mill Brewing Company is located on Grand Avenue, with plenty of people-watching and cool places to visit after your beer experience.

BEER LIST

Green Mill offers two seasonal beers at all times. Choices rotate every 4–6 weeks with 15–20 different seasonals annually. Some include Black Raven Bock in the spring, Grand Old Stone (hot rocks are actually added to the wort) in June and Pumpkin Ale in the fall (this is their most requested seasonal). Every six weeks a new beer is rolled out at "Roll Out the Barrel Night."

REGULAR TAPS

Gunflint Gold Ale
lots of carbonation giving it a thick head, slight malt taste, bitter finish, very refreshing

Knockadoon Irish Red Ale
perfect blend of sweet and bitter; toasted malt flavor

Grand Marais Pale Ale
sweet with hop undertones and a bitter finish. Keeps you coming back for more.

Big Island Porter
good all the way from start to finish. Deep red color with a buttery, roasted malt flavor.

SEASONALS

Raspberry Ale

summer seasonal. Raspberry and wheat used; fruit does not overpower the good beer flavor.

GREEN MILL PEPPER ALE SOUP

- **¾ c butter**
- **¾ c flour**
- **1 pint red ale or lager (more flavorful beer makes more flavorful soup!)**
- **1 pint golden ale or lager**
- **1 quart water**
- **2 T chicken base**
- **1 lb. cheddar cheese, shredded**
- **1 lb. pepper jack cheese, shredded**
- **4 oz. cream cheese, softened**
- **1½ tsp tabasco**
- **1 tsp salt**
- **¼ tsp cayenne**
- **4 oz. heavy cream**
- **croutons and shredded cheddar for garnish**

Melt butter in saucepan over medium heat and stir in flour. Turn heat to very low and cook for 3 minutes, stirring constantly. Set aside.

In a large pot bring beer, water and chicken base to a boil. Thicken with butter/flour mixture and turn off heat.

Add cheddar, pepper jack, cream cheese, tabasco, salt, cayenne and heavy cream. Heat slowly over low heat until hot. Garnish with croutons and a sprinkle of shredded cheddar. Excellent when paired with a Vienna-style lager or robust bock. Serves 10–14.

Address: 57 S. Hamline Avenue, St. Paul, MN 55105

Directions: From 94: exit on Hamline Avenue and head south to Grand Avenue; Green Mill is on the corner

Phone: (651) 698-0353

Hours: Monday–Saturday 11 am–1 am; Sunday 11 am–midnight; call to confirm

Website: www.greenmill.com

e-mail: stpaul@greenmill.com

THE HERKIMER
PUB & BREWERY

Location: Minneapolis

Owner: Blake Richardson

Brewmaster: Dave Hartmann

Founded: 1999

Annual production: 1,200 barrels

Price range of beers: around $4.00 per pint

Tours: not available

Tasting: only by the pint, but there is a guide available for those who may not know what to choose

Unique fact: The Herkimer is the only brewpub in the Uptown area of Minneapolis.

Events: annual golf tournament at Wild Marsh Golf Course in Buffalo, Minnesota, usually held in July

Amenities: parking and plenty of seating; on a nice day outdoor seating is available. Be sure to play a game of shuffleboard, you'll find it nowhere else.

Local attractions: the Lyn Lake neighborhood; Bryant Lake Bowling Alley and Theater complex (one of the coolest places on earth); Lake Street shopping; art galleries; Minnesota Center for Photography; The Jungle Theater; minutes from the Uptown area of Lake and Hennepin

ON TAP...

Owner Blake Richardson had an idea for a local pub that served great beer. Today that vision is a success. The Herkimer is the ultimate local hangout for a very eclectic neighborhood. Dark, warm, relaxed: a great place to chill.

The bar is decorated in a 1920s style, further adding to the laid-back attitude. The brewery is displayed in the dining area. Five fermenters dominate the space; a customer knows where the beer comes from. The bar features four taps that pour year-round and two seasonals.

The Herkimer offers a wide variety of menu items ranging from appetizers to entrees. Try the Spinach Parmesan Dip: lots of cheese and plenty of garlic served with bread; delicious! Employees of the Herkimer are very friendly and helpful. They will be able to answer your questions regarding the menu, beer and history. The large bar in the center of the Herkimer is conducive to a conversation among patrons. The Herkimer is a talking bar; people come here to hang out and visit. The feature of the Herkimer is definitely the people. Patrons are unique. All walks of life can be seen. Do not be surprised if you find new friends at the Herkimer.

BEER LIST

Other offerings you may find: Maibock, Oktoberfest, Alt, Kolsch, Dunkel Weiss, Vienna Country Bier, Doppelbock and Toolers Weiss.

REGULAR TAPS

Handy's Lager
traditional German lager. Light beer, good for the everyday beer drinker. Fruity finish.

Daily Pils
Czech-style pilsner. Light beer with a clean taste and finish; a thirst quencher.

High Point Dunkel
German dark beer. Chocolatey taste from the roasted malt.

Red Flyer Marzen
Oktoberfest-style beer served all year. Not your typical red beer; slight hoppy finish.

OTHER BREWS

Herkimer Root Beer
TripleCaff Energy Drink

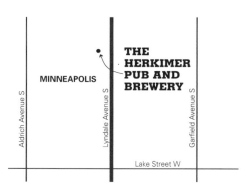

Address: 2292 Lyndale Avenue S, Minneapolis, MN 55408

Directions: from the north: follow 35W S; merge onto 94W (exit 17B); take the Lyndale Avenue/Hennepin Avenue exit (exit 231B); follow Lyndale Avenue S/N ramp; Herkimer is on the west side of the road

from the south: take 35W N; exit on 31st Street exit toward Lake Street; stay straight and go onto 2nd Avenue S; turn left on E Lake Street/County 3; turn right on Lyndale; Herkimer is on the west side of the road

Phone: (612) 821-0101

Hours: Monday–Friday noon–2 am; Saturday and Sunday 10 am–2 am; call to confirm

Website: www.theherkimer.com

e-mail: info@theherkimer.com

HOPS

Location: Maple Grove

Owners: Avado Brands, Inc.

Brewmaster: Ryan Walker

Founded: 1989; Maple Grove location opened in 1999

Annual production: about 500 barrels

Price range of beers: a pint costs around $3.75. Growlers cost close to $4.00 for the bottle and about $7.00 to fill. Customers can also join a Growler Club: fill nine growlers and your tenth is free.

Tours: just ask—usually one of the managers or brewmaster can oblige

Tasting: a sampler includes 6 4-oz. glasses and costs around $3.25

Unique fact: The Maple Grove site the first Hops to be opened in the state. Hops sends its spent mash from brewing to a local farmer. The Maple Grove site also sells the most beer out of all Hops nationwide.

Events: Happy Hour is Monday–Friday 3–7 pm; $1.00 off pints and bottled beers; 2-for-1 house wines, well and call drinks.
Late Night Happy Hour is 9 pm–midnight Monday–Saturday and features $3.00 specials of burgers, wings, potato skins and nachos. Pints, house wines and well drinks are $2.00.
Tapping Parties are held when Hops gets ready to roll out a new seasonal. Free samples of the new beer are given; there are also prize giveaways and specials on food.

Amenities: plenty of parking and seating; outdoor seating available; TVs; restrooms; souvenirs and brewing display; knowledgeable staff; food; kids' menu; wine and spirits; handicapped accessible. Can also accommodate parties up to 40.

Local attractions: Arbor Lakes shopping and events district: many shops and two movie theaters.

ON TAP...

The Hops franchise actually started in Florida in 1989. The restaurant was such a huge success that by the end of the 1990s there were 13 Hops restaurants operating in Florida. Over the past 15 years, Hops has grown to 72 restaurants in 16 states. Two were opened in Minnesota in late 1990s in Maple Grove and Eden Prairie. The Eden Prairie store closed, but the Maple Grove location continues to prosper.

Hops offers excellent beers, excellent food and a great atmosphere. What shines brightest is the people: they are friendly and willing to help you with anything. Hops is very laid-back. Many regulars frequent Hops, most for the excellent beer they offer. Brewing and beer memorabilia is featured throughout the bar.

BEER LIST

Hops features a variety of seasonals. The brewmaster is always formulating new recipes and bringing back old favorites. Other seasonals you might find include Hoptoberfest, Star Spangled Ale, Big 'Skeeter Pale Ale, Royal English Amber and Lumberjack Oatmeal Stout.

REGULAR TAPS

Clearwater Light
light and crisp with a light malt and hops finish. Excellent for first time microbrew drinkers.

Lightning Bold Gold
lighter ale, slight citrus and bitter flavor, smooth feel. Very good.

Thoroughbred Red
amber ale. More hops here, spice and citrus in the taste. Traditional ale flavor with a light red color.

Alligator Ale
dark ale. Thick and creamy, very malty. Nice balance in the end.

SEASONALS

Flying Squirrel Nut Brown Ale
great beer for the winter. Heavy, nutty flavor, smells wonderful.

Scottish Ale
packs a punch! Malty, thick and rich. Very complex flavor.

BEER BOILED SHRIMP

   1½ lbs. raw shrimp, deveined

   2½ c ale

   2½ c water

   ½ T kosher salt

   ½ tsp ground black pepper

   1 T Frank's Hot Sauce

   ¼ tsp chopped garlic

   ⅛ tsp crushed red pepper

Combine all ingredients except shrimp in a pot and bring to a boil over medium heat. Simmer beer mixture for 10 minutes. Add shrimp to pot and boil for 2 minutes, being careful not to overcook. Shrimp shells should be pink in color. Meat should be white and should slightly pull away from shell. Chill and serve with cocktail sauce and fresh lemon wedges.

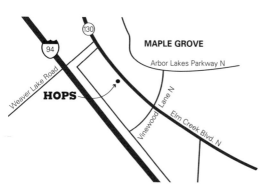

Address: 7855 Elm Creek Boulevard, Maple Grove, MN 55369

Directions: From 94: exit on Weaver Lake Road going east. Take a right and head south on Elm Creek Boulevard and look for the sign on your right.

Phone: (763) 416-1754

Hours: Monday–Saturday 11 am–1 am; Sunday 11 am–11 pm; call to confirm

Website: www.hopsrestaurants.com

e-mail: none available at time of printing

LAKE SUPERIOR
BREWING COMPANY

Location: Duluth

Owners: Dale Kleinschmidt, Don Hoag, JoAnne Hoag, John Judd, Karen Olesen

Brewmaster: Dale Kleinschmidt

Founded: 1994

Annual production: 2,000 barrels

Price range of beers: Check your local liquor store. You may be able to find taps at local bars and restaurants. The majority of Lake Superior's business is in bottles. Customers can find six packs and cases at their local liquor stores. Kegs are available but may be tough to come by.

Tours: Just give a call. Dale the brewmaster would love the opportunity. Visitors will most likely receive their first taste right from the bottling line.

Tasting: After taking the tour a sampling session is available. Any beers they are currently brewing or have bottled are yours to try. Included are their four year-round beers: Special Ale, Kayak Kolsch, Oatmeal Stout and Mesabi Red. Lake Superior does offer seasonals as well, such as Split Rock Bock, Marathon Wheat, St. Louis Bay I.P.A., Seven Bridges Brown Ale and Old Man Winter Warmer.

Unique fact: Duluth's only microbrewery.

Events: None hosted at the brewery itself, but the company is very active in the community. Lake Superior Brewing is involved in BockFest, Big Lake BrewFest, Gitchi

Gummi BrewFest and almost every event in the Duluth Area.

Amenities: small reception area featuring brewery facts and articles, display of ingredients and a small bar; restrooms

Local attractions: Tons! It's Duluth! Be sure to check out Canal Park, the Lift Bridge, the Lake Superior Maritime Visitor's Center, The Depot, the Great Lakes Aquarium and more. Take a boat ride and enjoy the beauty of the North Shore and Lake Superior.

ON TAP...

Lake Superior Brewing was founded in 1994. Originally located in the Fitger's complex, the brewery underwent two expansions. The second expansion, in 1998, saw the brewery move out of Fitger's to its own current location. The company started out small, brewing six-barrel batches only on Sundays. Currently the company is able to brew sixteen-barrel batches. Lake Superior Brewing was the first commercial brewer in the Duluth area after the original Fitger's closed in 1972. Their beers are made in small batches using the most traditional of methods. Ingredients include 100% malted barley and Lake Superior water. They use imported hops, American hops and imported yeast to give their beers very distinctive flavors.

Since opening they have expanded their territory to include the Duluth-Superior area, eastern Minnesota, northern Wisconsin, Minneapolis/St. Paul and Rochester. Lake Superior brews nine different beers annually. Four beers are available all year, and they also brew up to five seasonals. Lake Superior Brewing also offers an excellent Root Beer for the younger members of the family.

Lake Superior Brewing has won numerous awards. At the 2002 World Beer Championships in Chicago, Lake Superior took the following honors: Special Ale, Silver Medal; Mesabi Red, Silver Medal; Old Man Winter Warmer, Silver Medal; Kayak Kolsch, Silver Medal; Oatmeal Stout, Gold Medal.

BEER LIST

YEAR-ROUND BEERS

Special Ale
English pale ale. Lake Superior's flagship brew and best seller. Hoppy aroma and flavor, very good.

Kayak Kolsch German Ale
light and clean, slight malt flavor. Good one to start with.

Sir Duluth Oatmeal Stout
English style stout, dark and heavy. Chocolate and coffee tones with a roasted malt flavor.

Mesabi Red
American red ale; good red color. Marriage of malt and hops; higher alcohol content (6.5%).

SEASONALS

Split Rock Bock
dark and malty; five different roasted malts with a slight chocolate flavor

Windward Wheat
hefeweizen. Light and refreshing, serve with a lemon. Cloudy color and fruity flavor.

St. Louis India Pale Ale
lots of hoppy taste

Old Man Winter Warmer Barleywine
wine-like flavor; heavy on the tongue and a nice warming feeling. High alcohol content (10.3%).

Seven Bridges Brown
this is a lower-alcohol brown ale

OTHER BREWS

High Bridge Root Beer
very good

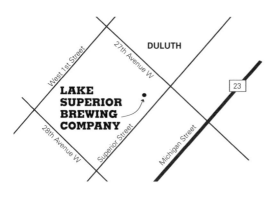

Address: 2711 W. Superior Street, Duluth, MN 55806

Directions: From 35: exit on 27th Avenue W; head to W. Superior Street; Lake Superior Brewing Company is located behind a Subway store; look for the office door with its insignia on the left of the building.

Phone: (218) 723-4000

Hours: Monday–Friday 10 am–4 pm; call to confirm; call ahead for a tour

Website: www.lakesuperiorbrewing.com

e-mail: info@lakesuperiorbrewing.com

MANTORVILLE BREWING COMPANY, LLC

Location: Mantorville (northwest of Rochester)

Owner: Tod Fyten, II

Brewmaster: Tod Fyten, II and assistant Todd Malo

Founded: 1996

Annual production: 1,000 barrels

Price range of beers: about $3.75 at the Hubbell House in Mantorville. Beers are only available on tap, mainly in the southern part of Minnesota, though bottling in 6-packs and growlers are planned for the future.

Tours: by appointment; be sure to call ahead and let Tod or Todd know. They will be happy to show you the operation.

Tasting: tastings are available on the tour

Unique fact: The current Mantorville Brewing Company is built on the ruins of the old Mantorville brewing company, which closed around 1939.

Events: Marigold Days is held the weekend after Labor Day and features events, live music, arts and crafts, 5K run, kids' fishing contest, street dance, truck show, parades and softball tournaments. Olde Tyme Days is the third Sunday in June and has a tractor pull, art show and more. Check out www.mantorville.com for more info.

Amenities: restrooms; a picnic area is planned; handi-capped accessible.

Local attractions: The Hubbell House is a 150-year-old

hotel located on the original stagecoach line from Winona and St. Peter. Very cool atmosphere and many original fixtures. The steaks are great! Dine in a place that has seen everyone from Ulysses S. Grant and the Mayo Brothers to Roy Rogers and Mickey Mantle. Downtown Mantorville is on the National Register of Historic Places. Many of the original buildings, including the original brewmaster's log cabin, still stand to this day. The Opera House still holds plays every weekend.

ON TAP...

The Mantorville Brewing Company is housed next to the Ginsberg Brewery, which was founded in 1858. Today the brewery is in its infancy, finding its legs and market. Tod Fyten purchased the complex from six local home brewers who used the facility. He has installed new fermenters and conditioning tanks. There are future plans for a new copper brew kettle and bottle filler to be installed within the next year. Todd is very active in the brewing community and is very knowledgeable about the industry.

If you're looking for Mantorville Brewing Company's beers, walk down the block to the Hubbell House or the Mantorville Saloon. Most of Mantorville Brewing Company's beers are featured in southeast Minnesota. With the installation of the new brewery and bottling equipment, Mantorville Brewing Company is actively working on expanding its market throughout Minnesota.

BEER LIST

Stagecoach Amber Ale
clean; malt and hops flavors are balanced. Very good stuff

Stagecoach Golden Ale
German "Kolsch" style ale. Slight honey taste; uses Minnesota honey

SEASONAL

Stagecoach Smoked Porter
made with whiskey malt, it has a very malty scotch flavor and a slight smokiness

Stagecoach Double Barrel Porter
bourbon cask conditioned smoked porter

STAGECOACH ROAST BEEF

4–5 lbs. pot roast of beef

2 T English mustard

seasoning to taste

2 T oil

1 large onion

½ pint Stagecoach Amber Ale

1 c sour cream

Spread meat with mustard and sprinkle with seasoning. Heat oil in a flameproof dish and brown beef quickly on all sides. Add onion and a little beer and simmer for 3–4 hours, adding more beer at intervals. Roast should be covered with liquid. Skim fat off of liquid and stir in sour cream just before serving. Serve with braised celery, glazed carrots and potatoes of your choice.

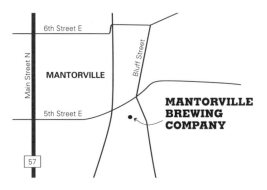

Address: 105 E. Fifth Street, P.O. Box 463, Mantorville, MN 55955

Directions: From Hwy 14, head north on 57 at Kasson to Mantorville. Once in Mantorville, head east on Fifth; the brewery will be on your right. If you go over the stream you have gone too far.

Phone: (651) 387-0708

Hours: call ahead to make an appointment for a tour

Website: www.mantorvillebeer.com

e-mail: tod@mantorvillebeer.com

MINNEAPOLIS
TOWN HALL BREWERY

Location: Minneapolis

Owner: Pete Rifakes

Brewmaster: Mike Hoops, who has ten years' experience. He and Dave Hoops from Fitger's are brothers. Mike and Dave both won awards at the 2004 Great American Beer Festival, the first time two brothers from different breweries won a medal in the same year.

Founded: 1997

Annual production: 1,000 barrels

Price range of beers: around $3.75 per pint, closer to $2.50 during happy hour. Growlers are available for about $13.00; refills are approximately $8.00.

Tours: by appointment, so please call ahead and they will be happy to accommodate you

Tasting: a house sampler with the five house beers is available for about $6.00; you can also get a seasonal sampler with five seasonal beers for around $6.00

Unique fact: Town Hall is the first brewpub in Minnesota to win a medal at the Great American Beer Festival. Also the Minneapolis Town Hall Staff is the current holder of the Great American Beer Festival Bowling Tournament Trophy. Minneapolis Town Hall Brewery is ranked as the 11th best brewpub in the U.S. by beeradvocate.com, a prestigious beer information site.

Events: Maibock Festival is the first weekend in May and features live music and the blessing of the bock. Anniversary Party during the third weekend in October. Live music, all beers plus a few special editions. August Pig Roast is an outdoor BBQ.

Amenities: restrooms; handicapped accessible; outdoor seating; bar and dining area; lounge area; full line of wines and spirits; full menu from appetizers to main course. Customers will find a knowledgeable staff when it comes to your beer questions. The brewmaster works with the staff on proper pouring techniques. A lifetime membership Pint Club is available for $125. Member benefits include free suds from 4–5 on Saturday, 75 cents off each pint, 2 Pint Club dinners per year.

Local attractions: University of Minnesota Campus; Cedar Avenue and the 7 corners area, which are full of ethnic shops and Cedarfest each summer. Downtown Minneapolis is just across the bridge. If you are headed to the Twins, Vikings, Gophers or Timberwolves, this a great place to start your game day.

ON TAP...

What does a person do when he wants to escape the corporate world? Open a brewpub! Pete Rifakes founded Minneapolis Town Hall Brewery in 1997. He wanted a place to call his own that served good food, excellent beer and a certain laid-back attitude.

Minneapolis Town Hall Brewery is a great place to meet a friend over a pint. A regular to the establishment will tell you Town Hall is a the place to relax and have a conversation. The brewpub is a nice break from the overbearing, loud bar-grill stereotype. The crowd is mixed. On game days Vikings, Twins, Gophers and Timberwolves fans can be found. The theater crowd will attend prior to a play. The atmosphere may change slightly at night when the students file in.

Minneapolis Town Hall Brewery is located in an old trolley station built in 1906. Hand painted portraits pay homage to brewing traditions of old. The ceiling and floors are original, adding lots of character. Everything about it says "take it easy and relax, have a conversation." Happy Hours are often, great deals on food and beer are offered. Minneapolis Town Hall Brewery offers excellent specials. The chef is creative and uses many of the beers in his cooking.

The beer at Town Hall is excellent. The brewmaster, Mike Hoops, uses Minnesota products as much as possible and has been known to experiment with centuries-old beer and ale recipes. For example, the Heather Ale is an old Scottish recipe using heather tips instead of hops; very unique. He has expanded his repertoire to barrel brewing, using wine and whiskey barrels to age the beers he crafts. These beers have a distinctive flavor due to the infusing of leftover characteristics of the barrel's previous contents. Town Hall offers five taps year-round and keeps three rotating seasonals. They usually release a new one every other week. A visitor will enjoy both pushed beers and cask drawn beers. Each cask lasts about two or three days. This is the ultimate neighborhood pub in the middle of the city. The majority of their business is regulars; after you visit, you're likely to become one too!

BEER LIST

REGULAR TAPS

Bright Spot Golden Ale
American ale, a light beer for the everyday drinker.

West Bank Pub Ale
English Pale Ale, uses English malt, yeast and hops in brewing. A little hop flavor. Amber in color.

Masala Mama India Pale Ale
very hoppy and sweet. The hop nose really hits you as you sip. #1 seller.

Black H20 Oatmeal Stout
smooth and creamy stout with a thick head. Chocolatey, malty flavor with hints of coconut and vanilla in the taste.

Hope and King Scotch Ale
smooth and crisp Scottish ale; slight hops, very unique

SEASONALS

Anniversary Ale
rich malty flavor, slight hops

Beer Engine Brown Ale
smooth and sweet, don't let this seasonal's dark color fool you

Seven English Style Bitter
seven English ingredients are used in this smooth and creamy bitter. Slight bitterness.

Heather Ale

Scottish ale made with Scottish malt and heather tips. Very interesting beer, herbal quality to the sweet flavor; no hops are harmed in the brewing of this beer.

CASK BEERS

West Bank Pub Ale

warmer temp gives a stronger, cask poured flavor. Slight cinnamon flavor.

Masala Mama India Pale Ale

a bitter that is smoother in texture with a stronger cask poured hop flavor

OTHER BREWS

Prohibition Pride Root Beer

great for the most discerning root beer customers

Address: 1430 Washington Avenue, Minneapolis, MN 55454

Directions: From 35: exit on to Washington Avenue and head east; Town Hall will be on your left; look for the hand painted mural next to the Holiday Inn.

Phone: (612) 339-8696

Hours: Monday–Saturday 11 am–1 am; Sunday 11 am–midnight; call to confirm

Website: www.townhallbrewery.com; updated often

e-mail: info@townhallbrewery.com

O'GARA'S BAR AND GRILL

Location: St. Paul

Owner: Dan O'Gara

Brewmaster: Larry Benkstein

Founded: 1941; brewpub opened in 1996

Annual production: 150–300 barrels

Price range of beers: about $3.75–$4.00 per pint. Growlers are available for around $12.75 and refills are approximately $9.25.

Tours: available upon request

Tasting: a sampler of 6 ales is available for around $5.00

Unique fact: Charles Schulz's (of Peanuts fame) father had his barbershop on the same corner. The original barbershop is now part of the O'Gara's complex.

Events: St. Patrick's Day is huge. Octoberfest each October. Guns and Hoses benefit for the St. Paul Fire Department. The Garage complex, a live music facility, hosts many local bands and local benefits.

Amenities: Plenty of parking and seating, outdoor seating available, restrooms. Knowledgeable staff, food, wine and spirits, kids' menu. Game room, TVs to catch your favorite sports team. Live music weekly. Handicapped accessible. Free shuttle bus to and from Vikings and Wild games. Banquet rooms and Garage can be rented for events.

Local attractions: Grand Avenue shops; Summit Avenue, home to the Governor's Mansion and many other historic homes plus a walking path; University of St. Thomas; Macalester College; Hamline University; not far from Como Zoo

ON TAP...

O'Gara's is a St. Paul institution. Many famous Minnesotans have walked through the O'Gara doors to enjoy a cold beer and a hot plate of food, including Matt Birk of the Minnesota Vikings and Joe Mauer of the Minnesota Twins. O'Gara's was founded by James Freeman O'Gara in 1941.

Charles Schulz's dad, Carl, had his barbershop next door. Charles and his family lived upstairs, and Charles called this place his home until he left in pursuit of his career. The current owner's father bought the place in 1972 and Dan O'Gara took over ownership in 2003. The commitment to keep the bar and restaurant in the family is one of the reasons O'Gara's is a great place.

From 1941 on, O'Gara's developed a reputation for good food and a friendly staff. O'Gara's is very active in the community as well. After 9-11 they hosted a fundraiser boullias (meat and veggie stew) cook-off in conjunction with the St. Paul Firefighters Association and the St. Paul Police Department. They raised over $279,000 for firefighters and police families in NYC. In return, a door from one of the wrecked fire trucks was sent from a New York City fire house and is now hanging up in the bar area.

O'Gara's is definitely an Irish bar. St. Patrick's Day is a week-long celebration. During that week O'Gara's also celebrates its anniversary. They boast the world's shortest St. Patrick's Day Parade as well, the entire parade route being 28 feet.

O'Gara's has gone through a number of expansions through the years, but hospitality is still the word here. The staff is very friendly. O'Gara's hosts a wide variety of customers, so the bar area is quite a place to hang out. There is a game room available, and a large room for parties and events. Customers can rent out the Garage for parties and receptions; in addition, there is a large seating area in the front that can also be reserved. The Garage hosts many local artists, and has become a Twin Cities hot spot for music. The front room features acoustic music and in the back O'Gara's Garage has rock bands and live music. You will not be disappointed visiting this classic neighborhood bar.

BEER LIST

Beers are brewed in seven-barrel batches. O'Gara's keeps four taps all year and has two seasonals that rotate. Seasonals you may get to try include Scotch Ale, Raspberry Lambic, Honey Brown, Oktoberfest, Winter Lager, Strawberry Blonde, Apricot Wheat, Altbier, India Pale Ale, Cream Ale and Amber Bock.

REGULAR TAPS

Cork Brown Ale
rich, dark ale; mild roast character from chocolate and caramel malts

Sligo Red
smooth malty flavor; medium hops character

Extra Special Bitter
very hoppy ESB; nicely balanced with sweet maltiness

Light Amber Ale
mild, smooth flavor

Sassy Sandy's Belgian Wheat
try it with a slice of orange—sassy!

SEASONALS

Scotch Ale
dark but mild with a hint of malt; lightly hopped

Address: 146 Snelling Avenue N, St. Paul, MN 55104

Directions: Exit from 94 on Snelling going south; get in the left lane. O'Gara's is on the corner of Snelling and Selby, three blocks from I-94. Parking is available on the south side of the building.

Phone: (651) 644-3333

Hours: Monday–Saturday 11 am–1 am; Sunday 11 am–midnight; call to confirm

Website: www.ogaras.com

e-mail: kris@ogaras.com

O'HARA'S BREWPUB AND RESTAURANT

Location: St. Cloud

Owners: Tim O'Hara

Brewmaster: Chris Laumb

Founded: 1945; brewpub added in 1996

Annual production: 600 barrels

Price range of beers: about $3.25 per pint, pitchers cost about $6.25. Growlers are available to take home for around $10.00; refills are approximately $8.00.

Tours: just ask; the brewing area is small, but the strength of the tour is speaking with the brewmaster

Tasting: A sampler of six beers costs about $5.25. A great deal! Included are the four regular taps and two seasonals.

Unique fact: O'Hara's was the first brewpub in St. Cloud, a city that once boasted a dozen breweries.

Events: St. Patrick's Day is huge—don't miss it

Amenities: plenty of seating and parking; restrooms; handicapped accessible; three full service bars; live music; banquet facilities and a huge downstairs game room

Local attractions: downtown St. Cloud; St. Cloud State Campus and St. Cloud State Huskies Division 1 hockey; Stearns County History Center; St. Cloud River Bat Minor League Baseball; Quarry Park, features trails connecting 21 abandoned granite quarries; golf; theater; Wheels, Wings and Water Festival

ON TAP...

Everyone in St. Cloud knows what establishment resides at 33rd and 3rd. O'Hara's is known for great food, good times and excellent brew. Truly a Minnesota institution. O'Hara's opened its doors in 1945. Original owner Cecil O'Hara bought an old grocery store on the outskirts of St. Cloud called Gus's and renamed it Cecil's. Cecil's brother Sid came home from the Navy and went into business with his brother and renamed the establishment Sid and Cecil's Little City. The store expanded in 1962 when the brothers purchased a liquor license and began to sell 3.2 beer out of the bottle shop. 1978 brought new owners and new vision. Sid's sons Tim and Mick revamped the store and created O'Hara Brothers Pub and Restaurant. In 1996 Tim expanded the bar and restaurant to house St. Cloud's first brewpub. The brewpub featured a new seating area, bar and event room. The brewery is visible behind a glass wall from this new wing. Enjoy a fresh glass of beer and watch the "chef under glass"—the brewmaster—as he works. Don't forget to have a basket of the best popcorn in the state!

BEER LIST

O'Hara's offers a wide range of seasonals depending on the time of year and the speed at which customers consume. A beer afficionado could find Hefeweizen, Raspberry Wheat (which is very raspberry!), Double Trouble, Maibock, Octoberfest, Pilsner and Winter Ale. All of their beers are brewed on site using the most authentic ingredients available. Belgian malts, and hops from Germany, Britain and the Pacific Northwest. O'Hara's Double Trouble won best of show at the Minnesota Craft Brewers Guild Winter Beer Festival.

REGULAR TAPS

Golden Honey Wheat
refreshing honey flavor in the finish; great summer or hot weather beer

Pantown Pale Ale
fruity hop flavor; bitter finish. Makes a pale ale drinker out of anyone!

Sid's Irish Stout:
chocolate and coffee tones; excellent. If you like stout, you will love it.

Quarry Rock Red
smooth, thick head, malty flavor

OTHER BREWS

O'Hara's Root Beer

BEER BATTER WALLEYE Recipe by Chef Dan Lunning

- **2 lbs. white flour**
- **1 T salt**
- **1 T black pepper**

Mix together and keep separate in 2"-deep pan

- **32 oz. O'Hara's Golden Honey Wheat Beer**
- **32 oz. (equal parts) "Fry Krisp" batter mix**

Mix beer and dry batter mix in a bowl with a wire whip. Yields ½ gallon batter.

Set your fryer to 350°. Dredge walleye fillets in seasoned flour, then put in batter mixture (you can put a toothpick at the tail end of walleye while putting in beer batter). Allow excess batter to drip off fillet. Submerge battered walleye in fryer oil and allow walleye to cook for 4–5 minutes (for 8-oz. walleye), or until golden brown. When walleye is done, place on paper towels to absorb excess oil. Serve with fresh tartar sauce. Note: You can also use jumbo shrimp for this recipe.

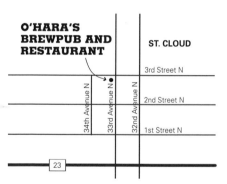

Address: 33rd and 3rd, St. Cloud, MN

Directions: From Hwy 23 (Division Street): turn north on 33rd Avenue and follow to 3rd Street; O'Hara's is on the corner.

Phone: (320) 251-9877

Hours: Monday–Saturday 11 am–1 am; Sunday 11 am–midnight; call to confirm

Website: www.oharasbrewpub.com

e-mail: laumb2@astound.net

ROCK BOTTOM BREWERY

Location: downtown Minneapolis

Owners: Rock Bottom Restaurants, Inc.

Brewmaster: Todd Haug

Founded: 1993

Annual production: 1,500 barrels

Price range of beers: pints are about $4.50; closer to $2.25 at Happy Hour. Growlers are available for around $7.95; refills are approximately $6.95.

Tours: tours are available

Tasting: A sampler of beers is available for around $6.10; included are five regular taps, one root beer and a sample of seasonal offerings. A great deal.

Unique fact: Rock Bottom is the only brewpub located in downtown Minneapolis.

Events: Rock Bottom offers its customers a mug club. Members enjoy a variety of benefits including invitations to Brewer's Dinners, special beer tappings and other events.

Amenities: restrooms; gift shop with souvenirs; separate bar and dining area; outdoor seating in the summer; game room with TVs; five tournament pool tables and darts; knowledgeable staff; very large menu of food, wine and spirits; brewing display; handicapped accessible. Accessible by the skyway system. Conference facilities for up to 60.

Local attractions: downtown Minneapolis; Target Center; Hennepin theater district and shops; connected to the skyway system

ON TAP...

Rock Bottom opened in 1993 with instant success. Rock Bottom uses a very simple model: great atmosphere, great food and great beer. The Minneapolis location is expansive. Customers can enjoy themselves in the dining room, bar or game room. The whole space is uniquely decorated with dark woods and retro light fixtures, which gives Rock Bottom a very welcoming atmosphere. The food is excellent and patrons will receive a big plate. You can even have a cigar from their own humidor. The staff is very friendly and willing to explain anything customers need to know. The bartenders are very knowledgeable about the beer they pour.

Rock Bottom has excellent beers! Todd Haug is a fine brewer. He spent time at Summit before taking the job at Rock Bottom. He has been brewing there for the past eight years. His beers are of superior quality.

Even though Rock Bottom is chain of breweries, each brewer is allowed to choose his own ingredients and brewing styles. Rock Bottom believes that each of their locations should have the freedom to tailor their beers to the local tastes. As a corporation, Rock Bottom breweries produce over 40,000 barrels of beer and have received over 60 medals for their beers. There are 29 Rock Bottoms in 15 states.

BEER LIST

REGULAR TAPS

Northstar Premium Lager
American lager. Rock Bottom's intro beer. Pilsen malt, light and crisp with a hint of honey.

Itasca Extra Pale Ale
totally awesome, has a slight caramel flavor, citrus flower aroma. Sweet and smooth, it's the bartender's favorite.

Erik The Red
Vienna style lager. Very smooth. Malty flavor, spicy hops taste and aroma.

Big Horn Nut Brown Ale
malty, dry finish. Raisin and cocoa flavor.

Rotating Dark Beer
dark and coffee-like with a chocolate flavor. Pushed with nitrogen.

SEASONALS

Anniversary India Pale Ale
lots of hops, and smooth fruit and citrus flavors

Winter Warmer
packs a punch! High alcohol warms you up, great for Minnesota winter. Sweet malt flavor.

Big Red
red ale. Hop flavor explodes.

OTHER BREWS

Superior Sarsaparilla
root beer made with honey and fresh lemon juice. Tastes of vanilla, sarsaparilla.

ROCK BOTTOM BROWN ALE CHICKEN

BROWN ALE JUS

14 oz. beef broth

14 oz. chicken broth

8 oz. brown ale

¼ c brown sugar

3 tsp balsamic vinegar

2 oz. butter

2 oz. all purpose flour

8 oz. heavy cream

Bring broths, ale, brown sugar and vinegar to a boil; simmer until liquid is reduced to about 18 ounces.

Melt butter in a separate pot. Add flour and stir until it thickens, approximately 3 minutes. Add 2 ounces of this roux to the broth/ale liquid and mix well. Add heavy cream. Bring to simmer and turn to low heat. Let cook for 4–5 minutes. Set sauce aside at room temperature.

WHITE CHEDDAR MASHED POTATOES

1½ gallons water

1 T salt

2½ lbs. russet potatoes, peeled, diced ½"

3 oz. heavy cream

2 oz. butter

¼ c sour cream

½ T salt

¼ tsp white pepper

4 oz. sharp white cheddar cheese, grated

Bring water in salt to boil in a large pot. Add potatoes and simmer until fork tender, approximately 15 minutes. Immediately drain potatoes into colander and allow to drain for several minutes until dry.

Place cream and butter into a container and heat in microwave until boiling.

Place potatoes back into pot and whip until the potatoes are smooth. Add sour cream and whip until just incorporated. Add seasoning and grated cheese and whip for 10 seconds. Add boiling cream mixture and whip until soft peaks form.

CHICKEN

½ c oil

⅛ c unsalted butter, plus 1 T

4 10-oz. chicken breasts

4 oz. Shiitake mushrooms

White Cheddar Mashed Potatoes

5 oz. Brown Ale Jus

Place chicken breasts, one at a time, in a plastic bag and pound with something heavy until they're about ¾" thick. Sprinkle with your choice of seasonings and set aside.

Place oil and ⅛ cup butter in a warm, oven-safe saute pan and blend together. Place seasoned chicken breast skin side down in saute pan and roast in 350° oven for about 4 minutes.

Flip chicken and add Shiitake mushrooms to pan around the chicken. Continue to bake for 4 more minutes or until chicken reaches an internal temperature of 165°.

Pile mashed potatoes in the center of a plate and keep warm. Remove chicken from pan and slice, then arrange the slices against the potatoes.

Pour Brown Ale Jus and remaining 1 T butter into the saute pan to deglaze. Cook until sauce is heated. Pour sauce over potatoes and chicken.

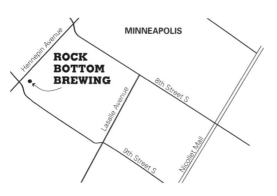

Address: 800 LaSalle Plaza, Minneapolis, MN 55402

Directions: Located on the corner of 9th and Hennepin in downtown Minneapolis.

Phone: (612) 332-2739

Hours: Monday–Thursday 11 am–1 am; Friday 11 am–2 am; Saturday 11:30 am–2 am; Sunday noon–midnight Happy Hour is Monday–Friday 2–6 pm; call to confirm

Website: www.rockbottom.com

e-mail: operations@rockbottom.com

SCHELL'S BREWING COMPANY

Location: New Ulm

Owner: family-owned

Brewmaster: Ted Marti

Founded: 1860

Annual production: 90,000 barrels

Price range of beers: check your local liquor store

Tours: Schell's tours are great; stop in the museum to purchase your tickets, $2.00 per person (children 12 and under tour for free). On holidays and weekends, arrive early to be sure that you get a spot. Private tours of 25 or more by special appointment. Tours given Memorial Day–Labor Day, Monday–Friday 2:30 pm and 4 pm, Saturday–Sunday 1 pm, 2 pm, 3 pm, 4 pm; off-season schedule from Labor Day–Memorial Day: Saturdays at 1 pm and 2:30 pm.

Tasting: at the end of the tour, you can sample six of Schell's beers

Unique fact: Schell's motto is "Never trust a brewery under 140 years old." The second-oldest family owned brewery in the United States, Schell opened when Abraham Lincoln ran for president.

Events: Bockfest is held the Saturday before Ash Wednesday, call for details. Live music, tours, German foods, bonfires and more. Search for the Bock Medallion. This is an outdoors event.
Oktoberfest is held the first and second weekend in October all over New Ulm. Lots of events, music and German food, also trolley rides in town.

HeritageFest is held the second and third weekends in July. Traditional German Music, five stages of performers, arts, crafts and much more. Check www.heritagefest.org. Brown County Fair is in August, held in New Ulm since 1867. New Ulm has many other annual events; check with New Ulm Chamber of Commerce for details.

Amenities: restrooms; gardens; hospitality room; gift shop; parking; brewing display; knowledgeable staff; deer park; museum; gift catalog; you can sign up for an email list. Oh, and watch out for the peacocks.

Local attractions: If you are going to visit New Ulm and are hungry, take my advice and go to the Kaiserhoff downtown and have the ribs—they are awesome! Be sure to visit Herman the German. Herman is a statue that overlooks the city.

ON TAP...

In 1848, German-born August Schell immigrated to the United States. He was 20 years old and trained as an engineer and machinist; owning a brewery was far from his mind. He bumped around from New Orleans to Cincinnati where he met his wife Teresa. In 1856 he, his wife and two daughters moved to southern Minnesota. Since many German immigrants had moved to New Ulm already, the move seemed natural to the Schells.

In New Ulm, August and a fellow named Jacob Bernhardt partnered to build a brewery in 1860. They could not have picked a more perfect location: an artesian spring provided the water, the Cottonwood River produced ice for storage, plenty of farm activity meant lots of raw materials, and the whole town was full of thirsty Germans. In that first year they brewed 200 barrels of beer.

Tensions between settlers and the Dakota Tribe flared up in 1862. During the Dakota Conflict much of New Ulm was razed to the ground with the exception of the Schell Brewery. Mrs. Schell was very generous with the Native Americans, sharing food and goods with them. Though it is only speculation, many believe that is why the brewery was saved.

Good fortune continued for August and family, and he bought out his partner in 1870. The brewery was officially Schell's Brewing Company. It was also in that same year that

August's son Otto took over for him when he became ill. A mansion was built on the brewery grounds for August and Teresa in 1885 for the huge sum of $5,000. The mansion still stands today. Six years later August passed away, giving ownership to his wife and son Otto.

Otto suddenly died in 1911, and control of the brewery passed to George Marti. George continued to run the business as usual until 1920, when Prohibition—The Noble Experiment—came into effect. Before Prohibition there were 1,900 breweries in the United States; at the end only 600 remained or reopened. Schell's was one of them. They were able to survive by producing soft drinks, tonic water, candy and near beer.

George Marti was not able to see his brewery grow after Prohibition was repealed. He died in 1934 and his son Alfred took over. Alfred was instrumental in creating the Schell's Hobo Band, which still tours and entertains today. Al retired in 1969 and his son Warren took the reins. Under his leadership Schell's expanded its product line to include 1919 Root Beer and Schell's Light. Warren was instrumental in keeping the Schell brewery alive and well during the rise of the Mega Breweries (Bud, Miller, Coors) of the 70s and 80s.

Current president and brewmaster Ted Marti took over in 1986. He was educated in brewing at the Siebel Institute in Chicago and spent time in Germany learning the craft. In 1990 Ted introduced a new line of beers to Schell family. These beers were more of the specialty ilk: Alt, Pilsner, Pale Ale and Hefeweizen. Today Schell's offers 16 different beers and contract brews 3 others. In 1999 the brewery added a state-of-the-art brewhouse, and in 2002 acquired Grain Belt, another historic Minnesota label, making Schell's the oldest and largest brewery in Minnesota.

The tour of Schell's is great. The Schell Brewing complex is on the Register of Historic Places. The people at Schell's have done a great job of keeping the brewery intact. The tour guides are knowledgeable about every aspect of history and current production. The tour starts with a short video highlighting the history of the brewery and the brewing process. The guide will pass around ingredients used in beer making for you to investigate. Next, a tour of the grounds highlights the history of each building. The original brewhouse still stands, as well as the home of August and family and the 1885 mansion. The gift shop was once a dormitory for workers. As you're guided through the brewhouse, check out the 104-year-old copper brewkettle, still used today. From there the guide will take you to the tasting room where you can sample six of Schell's beers. A small tasting guide is provided and the tour guide will give you specifics on each one. When your tour is over visit the gift shop for Schell apparel and many other unique gifts. Before or after the tour you are welcome to stroll, lollygag or meander about the gardens that surround the mansion.

BEER LIST

Schell's offers a wide variety of beers. What you taste at the end of the tour may depend on the season you visit. Year-round brews include Schell's Original, Schell's Light, Schell's Dark, Firebrick, Pilsner, Pale Ale, Caramel Bock, Grain Belt Premium and Grain Belt Premium Light. 1919 Root Beer is also made all year. Seasonal offerings change every few months and include Zommerfest, Octoberfest, Doppel Bock, Hefeweizen, MaiFest and Schmaltz's Alt. Schell's beers have won dozens of awards.

YEAR-ROUND BEERS

Schell Original
American lager, 140-year-old recipe. Light and crisp.

Schell Light
American lager, like the original but lighter.

Schell Dark
American lager, roasted malt gives the original a darker color and heavier malt taste.

FireBrick
Vienna-style lager, all barley malt used. Introduced in 1999 as a seasonal but because of demand moved to year-round production. Lightly hoppy, malty flavor, dark amber color.

Pilsner
Bohemian-style pilsner. Slight hop flavor, light color.

Pale Ale
German Pale Ale. Unique to Schell's, uses English hops and German yeast. Really hoppy malt finish. Brewmaster's favorite.

Caramel Bock
sweet and malty—my favorite

SEASONALS

Snowstorm
recipe changes each year; only the brewer knows its secrets

OTHER BREWS

1919 Root Beer

SAVORY GRILLED PORK ROAST IN SCHELL'S FIREBRICK MARINADE

4-lb. boneless pork loin roast, rolled and tied

5 garlic cloves, halved

MARINADE

12 oz. Schell's FireBrick Lager

¼ c olive oil

2 T butter

1 T dried basil

2 tsp marjoram

1 tsp sage

1 tsp rosemary

1½ tsp black pepper

1½ tsp salt

Cut 1" random slits in pork roast and stuff with halved garlic pieces. Place roast in a large sealable plastic bag. Mix the marinade ingredients in a bowl, pour into bag with the roast. Squeeze excess air from bag, seal and refrigerate overnight.

Using a charcoal grill, spread hot coals around outside edge of grill then add an additional layer of coals and you're ready to cook. Prior to grilling the roast, drain marinade from the bag and reserve for later. Place roast with meat thermometer in a baking pan, fat side up, and set baking pan in center of grill and cover. Be sure to keep a small amount of water in the bottom of pan to keep the roast tender. Generously baste the roast with the marinade every 15 minutes and continue to cook until temperature reads 160–165°. Let stand 10 minutes before carving, and spoon remaining marinade over the finished pieces.

For gas grills, place pan on top rack and follow same directions. For oven baking, set temperature to 325° and follow above directions.

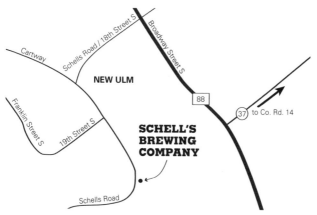

Address: 1860 Schell Road, New Ulm, MN 56073

Directions: From State Hwy 14, head south on County Road 37 into New Ulm. At the stop lights, head west on Broadway Street; get into the left lane right away. Head south on Schell's Road, follow the road past South Park and follow the signs.

Phone: 1-800-770-5020

Hours: Brewery Gift Shop: open daily 11 am–5 pm. August Schell Museum of Brewing: Free admission. Open Memorial Day–Labor Day, daily noon–5 pm; open off-season: Saturdays noon–3 pm, with exception during our Christmas Open House. Call ahead to confirm hours.

Website: www.schellsbrewery.com and www.grainbelt.com. The websites are very useful and updated often.

e-mail: schells@schellsbrewery.com

SUMMIT BREWING COMPANY

Location: St. Paul

President & Founder: Mark Stutrud

Brewmaster: Horace Cunningham

Founded: 1986

Annual production: 60,000 barrels with room to grow

Price range of beers: check your local liquor store for prices. Summit can be found in 6-packs, 12-packs, cases (all bottles) and kegs. During the holidays they offer a sampler pack—an excellent addition to any refrigerator!

Tours: Tuesdays and Thursdays at 1 pm. Saturday tours by reservation; call ahead as they fill up fast. Tour guides are very knowledgeable. The tour is the classic brewery tour, taking visitors through each step of the process.

Tasting: eight taps are available at the end of the tour; visitors are asked to enjoy a maximum of three in the Ratskeller

Unique fact: Minnesota's first new brewery to be built from the ground up in more than 100 years.

Events: none at the brewery, but Summit is featured at a number of events in the Twin Cities area

Amenities: Summit has a large Ratskeller and a gift shop

Local attractions: downtown St. Paul theaters; Xcel Energy Center; museums; West 7th Street shopping

ON TAP...

Mark Stutrud started Summit Brewing Company in 1986. At that time German and English style beers were almost nonexistent in the market, so Mr. Stutrud decided to found his own brewery. Summit first started in an old auto parts warehouse in St. Paul on University Avenue. A German brewhouse was imported to Minnesota and they were in business. The first keg of Summit was delivered to Johnny's Bar across the street on September 25th and the company has been off and running ever since.

Summit has grown quite substantially over the past fifteen years; by 1993 they had tripled their size. In 1998 they built a new brewery at the current location—the first newly built brewery in Minnesota in over 100 years. Quite an accomplishment, considering that 100 years earlier the state boasted some 120-plus breweries. In 2003, Summit expanded again, adding three new 450-barrel fermentation tanks.

Summit's business plan is to be the best regional brewery in the state. Finding a beer fan that has not had one of their brews would be a difficult task. The company has expanded to eleven states including Minnesota, Wisconsin, Iowa, Michigan, Kentucky, Indiana, North Dakota, South Dakota, Ohio, Nebraska and Illinois. Most of their sales come from the state of Minnesota. Summit has done this without the help of contract brewing, but they do contract one beer: Finnegan's Irish Amber. Finnegan's profits all go to a nonprofit group called the Spud Society. The Spud Society donates their funds to at-risk youth and the working poor in the Twin Cities area. The company is very active in the community and is engaged in numerous philanthropic undertakings. Summit is also featured at many outdoor events and festivals in the Twin Cities area. Customers can find Summit at the Minnesota State Fair, Grand Old Day in St. Paul, and Rock the Garden Festival, to name a few. Minnesotans can be proud to call this highly successful brewery their own.

BEER LIST

Summit offers four year-round beers and up to five seasonals

YEAR-ROUND BEERS

Extra Pale Ale

flagship beer, their best seller. British-style ale, bitter with a slight hop flavor. This beer established Summit as the regional brewery in Minnesota.

Grand Pilsner

Czech-style pilsner. Crisp and clean, lighter for the every-day beer drinker. Great thirst quencher.

India Pale Ale

English India pale ale. Lots of hops, excellent flavor.

Great Northern Porter

dark but light-bodied with coffee-like characteristics and a sweet finish

SEASONALS

Maibock

high alcohol, malty flavor, offered in the spring

Hefeweizen Wheat Beer

cloudy and light in color; smell of banana hits the nose before sipping. Citrus finish. Offered in the summer.

Oktoberfest Marzen

high alcohol, bronze color. Lager style with a smooth fin-ish, slight melding of malt and hops, excellent. Offered in the fall.

Winter Ale

sweet and warming; some say they can taste holiday spices in this winter seasonal

Oatmeal Stout

pushed with nitrogen for a creamy texture. Dark, slight coconut aroma, chocolatey flavor. Oatmeal Stout is a lim-ited release beer.

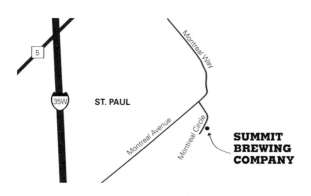

Address: 910 Montreal Circle, St. Paul, MN 55102

Directions: From 35 E North or South: Exit on Hwy 5 (West 7th Street); head west to Montreal Way; go south and follow to the brewery.

Phone: (651) 265-7800

Hours: Monday–Friday 8 am–5 pm; call to confirm

Website: www.summitbrewing.com

e-mail: info@summitbrewing.com

THEODORE FYTEN & ST. CROIX BREWING COMPANIES

Location: St. Paul

Owner: Tod Fyten, II

Brewmaster: Tod Fyten, II

Founded: Theodore Fyten Brewing Company, LLC was founded in 1999
St. Croix Brewing Company, LLC was founded in 1995

Annual Production: 1,000 barrels are produced by each brewing company

Price range of beers: Fytenburg beers are around $3.00–$5.00 on tap. Beers are only available on tap, mainly in St. Paul, though bottling in 6-packs and growlers are planned for the future.
St. Croix beers are about $4.50 at the Dock Café in Stillwater. Beers are available on tap, bottles and 6-packs, mainly in the St. Croix River Valley.

Tours: by appointment; be sure to call ahead and let Tod know. He will be happy to show you the operations

Tasting: tastings are available on tour

Unique fact: The current Theodore Fyten Brewing Company is built in the horse stables of the Stalhmann Brewery, which date back to the late 1850s.

Events: Look for Fytenburg beers at Grand Old Days, Taste of Minnesota and the St. Paul Winter Carnival. Check out Lumberjack Days and Taste of Stillwater for St. Croix beers.

Amenities: restrooms; a tasting room is planned

Local attractions: Glockenspiel, St. Paul's German restaurant, is located in the CSPS Hall (home to the Czech & Slovak Sokol), which dates to the 19th century. Very cool atmosphere. German appetizers are a specialty, and the Schweinhaxe is legendary. Xcel Energy Center

ON TAP...

The Theodore Fyten Brewing Company, LLC is housed in the horse stables of the Stahlmann Brewery, which was founded in 1855. Today the brewery is in the final build-out stages. Tod founded the brewery in 1999, and has been developing its brands along with his other brewery brands. He is installing a copper brew house, along with traditional open fermenters and conditioning tanks. There are plans for a bottle filler to be installed within the next year. Tod is very active in the brewing community and is very knowledgeable about the industry.

The St. Croix Brewing Company, LLC carries on a tradition of brewing in the Valley that dates back to the middle of the 19th century. The brewery was founded by a local St. Croix Valley homebrewer in 1995 and was purchased by Tod in 2003. Today the brewery is reestablishing its brands and finding its niche in the market. There are plans to add new flavors in the future.

If you are looking for St. Croix Brewing Company's products, most liquor stores in the Valley carry at least one of their offerings. The Dock Café in Stillwater and the Hammond Hotel in Hammond, Wisconsin, features St. Croix Maple Ale on tap.

BEER LIST

FYTENBURG BEERS

Tod is planning to add seasonals and limited production beers.

Fytenburg Export Ale
big, malty Dutch style golden ale

Fytenburg Weit Beer
delicate Dutch-Belgian white ale, using traditional Belgian ale yeast

ST. CROIX BEERS

St. Croix Maple Ale
America's original commercial Maple Ale

St. Croix Serrano Pepper Ale
America's original commercial Pepper Ale

St. Croix Cream Ale
an American original style first produced in the middle of the 19th century

FRENCH TOAST A LA CROIX

4 eggs

2 T brown sugar

$\frac{1}{2}$ c St. Croix Maple Ale

$\frac{1}{2}$ c milk

1 T cinnamon, divided

1 loaf French bread

butter or bacon grease

Whip eggs, then gently whip in brown sugar, St. Croix Maple Ale, milk and half the cinnamon. Slice French bread into $\frac{1}{2}$" slices. Soak bread in mixture on both sides, then fry on a hot griddle in butter or bacon grease. Add remaining cinnamon to egg mixture as more slices are dipped. Serve topped with butter and pure maple syrup.

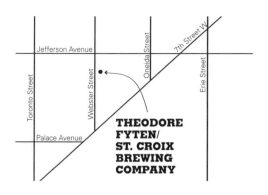

Address: 363 Webster Street, St. Paul, MN 55102

Directions: From Hwy 94 head south on Hwy 35 E to the Victoria Avenue exit. Take a left on Victoria and head 1 block to Jefferson Avenue. Take a left on Jefferson and proceed approximately 1 mile to Webster Street. Take a right and proceed ½ block.

Phone: (651) 387-0708

Hours: call ahead to make an appointment for a tour

Website: www.fytenburgbeer.com and www.stcroixbeer.com

e-mail: tod@fytenburgbeer.com and tod@stcroixbeer.com

UNION STATION 1ST CITY BREWERY AND GRILL

Location: Bemidji

Owner: Randy Ruttger

Brewmaster: Matt Tufto

Founded: 1997

Annual production: 500 barrels

Price range of beers: about $2.50–$3.75 depending on the size; around $2.00 for a pint during Happy Hour (4–7 pm and 9–12 pm)

Tours: yes, depending on the availability of the Brewmaster; call ahead to confirm times and dates

Tasting: a sampler of six beers (five regular taps and one seasonal) is around $3.75

Unique fact: Union Station is the only brewery in the United States north of the Mississippi River's headwaters.

Events: live music in the outdoor area during the summer; Boreal Brewers (the local brewing association) holds tastings Fall and Spring—check on dates, but this is open to the public; Bemidji State University Homecoming; Fourth of July Water Carnival

Amenities: handicapped accessible; restrooms; outdoor seating; conference facilities; separate bar and dining area; game room; free parking; TV (catch the sports!); wine and spirits; kids' menu; great variety of food; knowledgeable staff. Union Station also offers a mug club to its customers. Currently there are about 200 members. Benefits include your first beer free and 8 oz. extra per pour.

Local attractions: Bemidji State University; lakes and resorts; fishing, golf and Northwoods camping at state parks and state forests; Paul Bunyan and Babe statue—one of the most photographed spots in the United States

ON TAP...

Union Station 1st City Brewery and Grill is housed in Bemidji's original Union Train Depot, hence the name. The station was built in 1911 and was used for almost the next 60 years. The last passenger train left in 1967. The majority of the structure is original with the exception of the brewery, restrooms and kitchen. The carriage entrance is now the garden court. The station lobby was converted to the dining room, and the express area is now the bar. The decor is fantastic: original chandeliers, light fixtures and wood. Be sure to check out the ticket booth in the bar area. Train memorabilia is displayed throughout. Simply walking in takes a customer back to the bustling train station of years gone by.

The Union Station offers a full menu from appetizers to entrees. The burgers are big and the nachos are too. Food can be ordered in the bar area or dining area. If you are planning on dinner in the dining room in the evening, it's best to call ahead for reservations. Union Station is a destination restaurant for all special occasions, anniversaries, birthdays, etc. The atmosphere at Union Station is very cool; it is gorgeous. The bar area is laid-back—good for a conversation. At night things pick up when the college crowd comes by. The clientele is a mix of Bemidji natives, business people, working people, families and students. Lots of space for your favorite bar game and free popcorn to boot!

Union Station employs a four-barrel brewing system. The brewer, Matt Tufto, takes great care in his brewing. He started brewing from scratch at the Union. The previous brewer showed him the ropes twice and he was off and running. He brews beers that are clear and crisp, pleasing to the beer fan but also to the everyday customer. Union Station uses German and English hops and grains when brewing.

BEER LIST

Five taps are offered year-round. Seasonals are offered as well; they rotate as fast as they are sold and include Molasses Ale, Oatmeal Stout, Kolsch, Cranberry Ale, Cherry Wheat and Ginger Ale. Union Station uses Minnesota products whenever possible. The 1st Street Wheat contains honey from a local beekeeper.

REGULAR TAPS

1st Street Wheat
light beer, easy to drink, a good starter. Wheat and honey meld together for a great flavor.

Golden Spike Ale
pale ale, smooth and clean, fruitiness of the hops comes forward, slight citrus

Cannonball Red
two row malt, reddish brown color. Hop smell, slight caramel flavor.

Orient Express India Pale Ale
a mellow IPA, very good. Hops definitely.

Coal Train Porter
very good, dark coffee undertone

SEASONALS

Molasses Ale
dark and thick, high alcohol; molasses comes through at the end

Oatmeal Stout
coffee and chocolate, warming affect. Malty flavor and dark.

UNION STATION BBQ SAUCE BREAD STARTER

5 lbs. wild rice

4 lbs. brown sugar

3 gallons water

1 gallon Golden Spike Ale

1 gallon stone ground mustard

Heat all ingredients on medium-low heat until rice begins to open. Slowly cool and refrigerate. Lasts forever.

WILD RICE BREAD

- **½ gallon Union Station BBQ Sauce Bread Starter**
- **1 lb. lard**
- **½ gallon hot water**
- **3 c sour cream**
- **6 oz. yeast**
- **1 T salt**
- **8 lbs. white flour**
- **2 lbs. wheat flour**

Microwave bread starter and lard for 3 minutes. Mix hot water and sour cream in. Add yeast and salt, mix in flour until dough is workable, let rise before dividing into 15 equal portions. Let rise and bake at 200. Makes 15 loaves.

Address: 128 1st Street, Bemidji, MN 56601

Directions: From MN 197: Turn left on 2nd Street NW; turn left on Bemidji Avenue N; turn right on 1st Street W; Union Station is on the left

Phone: (218) 751-9261

Hours: Monday–Saturday 11 am–1 am; Sunday 11 am–midnight; call to confirm

Website: under construction

e-mail: station@paulbunyan.net

VINE PARK BREWERY

Location: St. Paul

Owners: Andy Grage and Dan Justesen

Brewmasters: Andy Grage and Dan Justesen

Founded: 1995

Annual production: roughly 925 barrels; amount produced depends on their customers

Price range of beers: Average batch of beer is about $125, plus a first-time bottle charge of about $45 for bottles (bottles are reusable). For that amount, a customer gets 72 22-oz. bottles of their very own brew.

Tours: come on in; they are happy to show you around

Tasting: you get to taste what you brew

Unique fact: Vine Park is the only place in the Midwest that allows customers to brew their own beer and wine.

Events: Octoberfest features a grill and tent outside, and massive bottling going on inside. Vine Park's Summer Brews Cruise is a riverboat cruise on the Mississippi; six different beers offered, plus brats and chicken on the grill and a free glass to boot. Call for details.

Amenities: knowledgeable staff; restrooms; handicapped accessible

Local attractions: downtown St. Paul theaters; Xcel Energy Center; museums; West 7th Street shopping

ON TAP...

Okay, you have gone to every brewpub and brewery in the book. Now what? How about brewing some of your own? Vine Park is the place to go. Vine Park is a brew-on-premises establishment; basically this means they will provide you with the ingredients and the know-how and you supply the man-power. The staff (Andy and Dan) will take you from brewing to bottling, and no matter how hard you may try to ruin your beer, they will not let that happen. Both have degrees from the World Brewing Academy and are certified beer judges. Andy and Dan have received home brewing awards. They know what they are doing.

Customers make a reservation to come in and brew. A list of 50 different recipes is offered to choose from. Brewing takes about one and a half to two hours. Bottling takes place two weeks later. There are six brewing kettles available. Vine Park asks customers to limit three people to a kettle. If you reserve all six kettles, they will allow a maximum of five people per kettle.

On Wednesday nights Vine Park hosts a Brew Club. They will host up to twelve people at a discounted rate. The group will brew six different batches of beer that night, then return two weeks later to bottle. The cost is around $60 per person plus $21.60 for bottles and you walk away with 36 22-oz. bottles of beer.

If you're looking to get a bunch of people together Vine Park is a great idea. Great for sales awards, corporate and family outings. Instead of the same old golf outing or family picnic, take them brewing! For those of you who are not beer fans, but are fans of the winery portion of the book, Vine Park also offers winemaking. Check it out!

(On a personal note I know what I will be writing on my list for Christmas next year.)

BEER LIST

Vine Park's recipe list is 50 recipes long. These are Vine Park's most popular recipes.

Loose Moose Lager

the light companion to Vine Park's Dark Moose. It's pale gold in color with a distinctive hop and mild malt flavor.

Red Hyena Ale

a light-bodied amber ale with a subtle hop and malt flavor and a dry finish

Walnut Brown Ale

medium-bodied ale, mildly hopped with a slight coffee flavor

Address: 1254 W. 7th Street, St. Paul, MN 55102

Directions: From 35 E: exit on West 7th Street and head east. Vine Park will be on your right, approximately 4 blocks from 35.

Phone: (651) 228-1355

Hours: Reservations Monday–Friday for 11 am, 1:30 pm, 4 pm and 7 pm; Saturday 9 am, noon, 3 pm and 6 pm. Wednesday night Brew Club starts at 7 pm. Bottling appointments are exactly two weeks after brew date at approximately the same time. Call ahead to confirm.

Website: www.vinepark.com; this is an excellent website

e-mail: andy@vinepark.com or dan@vinepark.com

WELLINGTON'S BACKWATER BREWING COMPANY

Location: Winona

Owners: Geoff Gardner

Brewmaster: Chris Gardner

Founded: 1995

Annual production: 350 barrels

Price range of beers: pints are around $3.00; a pitcher costs about $7.00. Growlers are available Monday–Saturday 10 am–10 pm and cost about $11.99; refills are approximately $7.99.

Tours: Just ask, best to call ahead for any of the brewery staff. Chances are you will see the brewery in action—Backwater brews two batches a week.

Tasting: sampler is around $4.00; includes four regular taps, a seasonal and the root beer

Unique fact: First brewery in the Winona area since Bub's closed in 1960. The only brewpub in the state that also features a bowling alley.

Events: The home brewing contest is usually held in February or March; call for details. This contest is open to the public for tasting. The Winter Polka Fest usually takes place in December or January; call for details. This is the "rollout" for the winter seasonal, and the brewmaster plays the accordion too.

Amenities: plenty of parking; free popcorn; jukebox; bowling alley; game room; TVs; restrooms; wine and spirits;

food; kids' menu; brewing display; knowledgeable staff; handicapped accessible

Local attractions: the Mississippi River and Bluff Country; Winona State University; historical downtown Winona; St. Mary's University; plenty of golf courses

ON TAP...

Wellington's Backwater Brewing Company, Grill and Westgate Bowl were built in the 1960s when the bowling alley opened. The brewmaster, Chris Gardner, first offered his home-brewed selections in 1988 on St. Patrick's Day. The popularity of his homebrews inspired the owners to add a brewpub in 1995.

The new pub signified the first brewery in Winona since 1960 and resurrected a once-proud brewing tradition. At one time in its history Winona boasted eight breweries. Chris went to brewery school at the Siebel Institute in Chicago and began brewing full-time at Backwater. The brewery was found for sale in Michigan and brought back by truck to Winona. Space was added for the kettles, which are old soup kettles. Each is forty gallons and is excellent for boiling. The next year they added some new equipment: two fermenters and carbonation tanks from Oregon.

Wellington's is a classic sports bar that serves some excellent beers. Memorabilia is featured as decor. The clientele are locals, sports fans, college students and travelers from Highway 61 headed to Minnesota's Bluff Country. Do yourself a favor and follow Highway 61 to Winona; it is gorgeous. The bar/grill features a full menu and its own smokehouse—the ribs are excellent. They also make their own barbecue sauce. If you are hungry, the burgers are cooked over an open flame and they are big!

Their beers have earned many fans in the area. At first, the lighter beers were the best sellers, but according to Chris, the more traditional beer recipes have now won over the regulars. The staff is also very knowledgeable about the beers and are excited to give you a taste if you are not sure about which one to choose.

BEER LIST

The beers are unpasteurized and unfiltered. They brew often—a fresh pint is always available. The beers reflect the tastes of Minnesota and use many Minnesota ingredients.

REGULAR TAPS

Cat Tail Pale Ale
American-style pale ale, copper color with a slight taste of caramel. Definitely a hoppy flavor, rich and creamy.

Rivertown Nut Brown Ale
best seller. Sweet and malty, slight nut flavor. Great beer for someone not used to drinking dark beers.

Bullhead Red Ale
dry and malty. Red color, smooth but with lots of flavor.

Wing Dam Wheat
Kolsch style. Cloudy color with a smooth finish. Light hops; really easy to drink.

SEASONALS

Steamboat Stout
caramel and coffee flavor. Fall/winter seasonal. Roasted oats used in brewing; very dark, very malty.

OTHER BREWS

Backwater Brewing Company Root Beer
old style root beer

BACON BIER CHEESE

6 quarts water

2 pints Backwater Brewing's Wing Dam Wheat

1 lb. bacon

5 T chicken base (preferably Minor's)

1 tsp granulated garlic

2 tsp white pepper

1 lb. butter

3 c flour

8 oz. American cheese

2 oz. Swiss cheese

2 oz. shredded mozzarella cheese

Add water and beer to a 10-quart pot and boil for 15 minutes making sure all alcohol is boiled out. (Leaving alcohol in gives a bitter flavor.) While water is boiling, fry the bacon and cut into 1" pieces. Add bacon, chicken base, garlic and white pepper to boiling water. In a separate sauce pan or microwave oven, melt the butter and slowly whisk in the flour until it reaches a smooth consistency. Set aside. Now stir the cheeses into the soup. You must keep stirring the soup to prevent burning. Once all the cheese is in and completely melted, take the soup off heat. Immediately add the melted butter/flour mixture to the soup kettle and stir in completely. Now enjoy!

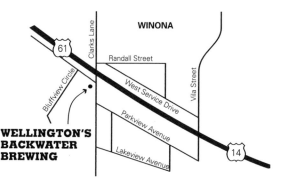

Address: 1429 W. Service Drive, Westgate Shopping Center–U.S. 61, Winona, MN 55987

Directions: From Hwy 61 head south on W. Service drive, then take a left. Wellington's Backwater Brewing Company will be on your right. Plenty of signage on the way, easy to find.

Phone: (507) 452-2103

Hours: Monday–Saturday 11 am–1 am; call to confirm

Website: sorry, no website available at time of printing

e-mail: ccgardy@rconnect.com

WINERIES

- Alexis Bailly Vineyard, Hastings
- Cannon River Winery, Cannon Falls
- Carlos Creek Winery, Alexandria
- Falconer Vineyards, Red Wing
- Fieldstone Vineyards, Morgan
- Forestedge Winery, Laporte
- Luedke's Winery, Princeton
- Minnestalgia Winery, McGregor
- Morgan Creek Vineyards, New Ulm
- Northern Vineyards, Stillwater
- Saint Croix Vineyards, Stillwater
- Scenic Valley Winery, Lanesboro
- Two Fools Vineyard & Winery, Plummer
- WineHaven Winery and Vineyard, Chisago City

NEW WINERIES

- Crofut Family Winery & Vineyard, Jordan
- Diamond Ridge Winery, Peterson
- Post Town Winery, Rochester

BREWERIES

- Bandana Brewery, Mankato
- Barley John's Brew Pub, New Brighton
- The BrauHaus, Lucan
- Fitger's Brewhouse Brewery and Grille, Duluth
- Gluek Brewing Company, Cold Spring
- Granite City Food and Brewery, St. Cloud and Maple Grove
- Great Waters Brewing Company, St. Paul
- Green Mill Brewing Company, St. Paul
- The Herkimer Pub & Brewery, Minneapolis
- Hops, Maple Grove
- Lake Superior Brewing Company, Duluth
- Mantorville Brewing Company, Mantorville
- Minneapolis Town Hall Brewery, Minneapolis
- O'Gara's Bar and Grill, St. Paul
- O'Hara's Brewpub and Restaurant, St. Cloud
- Rock Bottom Brewery, Minneapolis
- Schell's Brewing Company, New Ulm
- Summit Brewing Company, St. Paul
- Theodore Fyten & St. Croix Brewing Companies, St. Paul
- Union Station 1st City Brewery and Grill, Bemidji
- Vine Park Brewery, St. Paul
- Wellington's Backwater Brewing Company

Norm Ayen grew up in a small town in southern Minnesota. After high school he spent four years in the U.S. Air Force and then attended Minnesota State-Mankato where he graduated with degrees in English, Physical Education and Health. He recently retied after 32 years of teaching and coaching. He is now living in Maryland with his wife Judy where he coaches track and field.

Shane Weibel is a Social Studies teacher. He lives in Cambridge, Minnesota with his wife Tina, son Kellen, and Basset Hound Luther. He has a Bachelor of Science in Social Studies Education with a History Emphasis from St. Cloud State University and a Masters of Science in Educational Leadership from Southwest Minnesota State University.